Unbelievably Good Deals
& Great Adventures
That You
Absolutely Can't Get
Unless You're Over

50

Unbelievably Good Deals
& Great Adventures That You Absolutely Can't Get Unless You're Over
50

JOAN RATTNER HEILMAN

CB

CONTEMPORARY
BOOKS

CHICAGO · NEW YORK

Library of Congress Cataloging-in-Publication Data

Heilman, Joan Rattner.
   Unbelievably good deals and great adventures that
you absolutely can't get unless you're over 50.

   Includes index.
   1. Travel.   2. Discounts for the aged.   I. Title.
G151.H44   1988   910′.02   88-377
ISBN 0-8092-4705-4

Published by Contemporary Books, Inc.
180 North Michigan Avenue, Chicago, Illinois 60601
Manufactured in the United States of America
Library of Congress Catalog Card Number: 88-377
International Standard Book Number: 0-8092-4705-4

Published simultaneously in Canada by Beaverbooks, Ltd.
195 Allstate Parkway, Valleywood Business Park
Markham, Ontario L3R 4T8 Canada

Contents

Unbelievably Good Deals
& Great Adventures
That You
Absolutely Can't Get
Unless You're Over
50

Chapter One

Introduction to Good Deals and Great Adventures

This book is for people who love to do interesting things and go to new places—and don't mind saving money while they're doing it. It is a guide to the perks, privileges, discounts, and special adventures to which you have become entitled simply because you've hung in there for 50 years.

On your 50th birthday, you qualify for hundreds of special opportunities and money-saving offers that will have lots of people wishing they were older. All for a couple of good reasons. First, you deserve them, having successfully negotiated your way through life's white waters. And second, as the fastest-growing segment of the American population, you represent an enormous market of potential consumers, a fact that has become quite apparent to the business community. More than a quarter of the U.S. population today is over 50. One out of every eight Americans is over 65, outnumbering teenagers for the first time in history. Besides, life expectancy is higher today than ever before, and most of us can expect to live a long, healthy, and active life.

Those of us over 50 control most of the nation's wealth, including half of the discretionary income, the money that's left over after essentials have been taken care of, and 80 percent of the savings. For most of us, the children have gone, the mortgage has been paid off, the house is fully furnished, leaving large inheritances is not a major concern, and the freedom years have arrived at last.

As a group, we're markedly different from previous older generations, who pinched pennies and saved them all. We, too, know the value of a dollar, but we feel freer to spend our money because we're better off than our predecessors, a significant number of us having accumulated enough resources to be reasonably secure. We also are far better educated than those before us, and we have developed many more interests and activities.

And, most important, we as a group are remarkably fit, healthy, and energetic. We are in *very* good shape—and feel that way. In fact, a survey has shown that most of us feel at least 15 years younger than our chronological age.

The business community is actively courting "the mature market," as we are known, because now we have the time and the money to do all the things we've always put off. Because of the new recognition of our numbers, our flexible schedules, and our vast buying power, we are finally being taken very seriously. To get our attention, we are increasingly presented with some real breaks and good deals, all of which are detailed on these pages. We are also invited on trips and adventures specifically oriented toward our interests, needs, and abilities. You will find them here too.

In this book, you will learn how to get what's coming to you—the discounts and privileges you couldn't get if you were younger:

▶ The discounts at hotels and motels, at car-rental agencies, on buses, trains, and boats
▶ The best money-saving offers from the airlines that are eager for your patronage
▶ The colleges and universities that offer you an education for free—or nearly
▶ The insurance companies with discounts for people at 50 or thereabouts

▶ The trips, domestic and foreign, designed specifically for the mature market
▶ The free passes to all the national parks
▶ The ski resorts where you can ski for half price—or for nothing
▶ The tennis tournaments, road races, biking events, and beauty contests you may enter
▶ And much more!

Because every community has its own special perks to offer you, make a practice of *asking* if there are breaks to which you are entitled wherever you go, from movies to museums, concerts to historic sites, hotels to ski resorts, restaurants to riverboats, in this country and abroad. Don't expect clerks or ticket agents, tour operators, restaurant hosts, even travel agents to volunteer them to you. First, they may not think of it. Second, they may not realize you have reached the appropriate birthday. Third, they may not want to call attention to your age, just in case that's not something you would appreciate!

Remember to request your privileges *before* you pay or when you order or make reservations, and always carry proof of age or an over-50-club membership card, or, better yet, both. Sometimes the advantages come with membership, but often they are available to anyone over a specified age.

With the help of this guidebook, you will have a wonderful time and save money too. Enjoy!

Chapter Two
Travel: Making Your Age Pay Off

People over 50 are the most ardent travelers of all. They travel more often, farther, more extravagantly, and for longer periods of time than anybody else. Ever since the travel industry discovered these facts, it's been after our business.

It's fallen in love with our age group because we have more discretionary income than people of other ages. And because we are wonderfully flexible. Many of us no longer have children in school, so we're free to travel at off-peak times or whenever we feel we need a change of scenery. In fact, we much prefer spring and fall to summer. Some of us have retired or have such good jobs that we can make our own schedules. We can even take advantage of midweek slack times when the industry is eager to fill space.

But, best of all, we are energetic, and we're not about to stay home too much. People over 50 account for about one-third of all domestic travel, air trips, hotel/motel nights, and trips to Europe and Africa. Nine out of 10 of us are experienced travelers and savvy consumers.

Contrary to what a yuppie might think, people in the over-50 generation aren't content with watching the action; we like to get right into the middle of it. There's not a place we won't go or an activity we won't try. Though many of us prefer escorted tours, almost half of us choose to travel independently.

Not only that, but we're shrewd—we look for the best deals to the best places. We are experienced comparison shoppers and seek the most for our money.

For all these reasons, we are now offered astonishing numbers of travel-related discounts and reduced rates as well as special tour packages and other perks. Many agencies and tour operators have oriented all or part of their trips toward a mature clientele. Others include older travelers with everyone else but offer us special privileges.

Many of the airlines have formed travel "clubs" specifically for older travelers, giving discounts to members who pay a small membership fee to join, or offer passes for a year of travel for one-time payments. Sometimes they give discounts for midweek travel to certain destinations. And most of the hotel and motel chains—as well as individual inns and hotels—now offer similar inducements, such as discounts on rooms and restaurants.

There are so many good deals and great adventures available to you when you are on the move that we'll start right off with travel.

But, first, keep in mind:

▶ Rates, trips, and privileges tend to change at a moment's notice, so check out each of them before you make your plans. Airlines and car-rental agencies are particularly capricious, and it's hard to tell what they offer from one week to the next. The good deals in this guidebook are those that are available as we go to press.

▶ Always ask for your discount when you make your reservations or at the time of purchase, order, or check-in. If you wait until you're checking out or settling your bill, it may be too late.

▶ Also remember that discounts may apply only between certain hours, on certain days of the week, or during specific seasons of the year. Check this out before making reservations and always remind the clerk of the discount when you check in or pay your fare.

▶ It's particularly important when traveling to carry

identification with proof of age or membership in an over-50 organization such as AARP or Mature Outlook (see Chapter 20). In most cases, a driver's license or passport does the job. So, in some cases, does the organization's membership card, as well as a birth certificate, a resident alien card, or any other official document showing your date of birth. If you're old enough for a Medicare card or Senior ID card, use that.

▶ Don't always spring for the over-50 discount without checking out other rates. Sometimes special promotional discounts available to anybody any age turn out to be better deals. The railroads, for example, are famous for this. Ask your travel agent or the ticket seller to figure out the *lowest possible available rate* for you at that moment.

▶ If you belong to an organization like AARP or Mature Outlook (see Chapter 20), some of these bargains are yours at age 50. Others come along a little later at varying birthdays, so watch for the cutoff points. Also, in many cases, if the person purchasing the ticket or trip is the right age, the rest of the party or the people sharing the room are entitled to the same reduced rates.

Chapter Three
Out-of-the-Ordinary Escapades

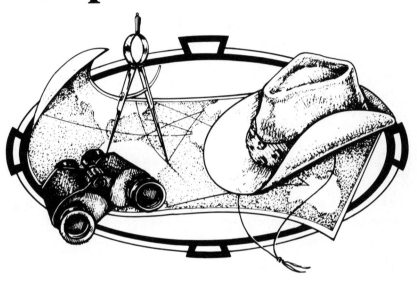

If you are an intrepid, especially energetic, perhaps even courageous, sort of person who's intrigued by adventures that don't tempt the usual mature traveler, take a look at these possibilities. They are all designed to give you tales with which to regale your friends, relatives, and acquaintances—at least until you embark on the next one!

AMERICAN YOUTH HOSTELS

The outfit that disperses teenagers on low-cost bike trips all over the world is not for youth alone. In fact, it offers an array of inexpensive adventures—bike tours and otherwise—specifically to people over 50. And, of course, older people are invited to go along on any AYH trips labeled "for adults." A recent cycling trip to New Zealand, for example, had an age range of bikers from 23 to 70.

If you want to go on an AYH adventure trip, you must become a member. Membership is $20 a year, unless you've reached 60, in which case you pay only $10. Members get a card and a guidebook that lists hostels in the United States. You may purchase handbooks for Europe and other areas of the world.

The U. S. affiliate of the International Youth Hostel Federation that coordinates more than 5,000 hostels in 64 countries, the AYH has been operating for over half a century. Each of its trips is limited to 10 participants, including the trip leader. You'll stay primarily in hostels, which are inexpensive dormitory-style accommodations, no two of which are alike. You might stay in a castle in Germany or a lighthouse in California or a budget motel in Massachusetts. Most hostels have kitchens where your group prepares its own meals; a few have cafeterias.

Each year, AYH plans six itineraries especially for the over-50 crowd, including hiking or cycling tours, motor trips, and a train trip. The current roster offers a 9-day camping and cycling trip through the cheese country of Wisconsin; two weeks on a mini-van tour through five New England states in the fall foliage season; 9 days of cycling in New England in the fall; 16 days by van in the Pacific Northwest; five weeks by train and ferry through the major countries of Europe; and 16 days by public transportation on an Oktoberfest tour of Bavaria.

In addition to all that, you are entitled to lodge at any youth hostel in the world, including the new network of urban hostels now in Chicago; Washington, D.C.; New York; Boston; San Francisco; Miami Beach; New Orleans; and Los Angeles (one night's stay costs $4 to $10). There is no maximum age limitation for booking a bed in these wonderfully cheap lodgings and to hobnob with other hostelers who prefer not to pay exorbitant hotel prices. Be ready, however, to sleep in a double-decker cot in a sex-segregated dormitory for about six or eight people supervised by "hostel parents."
For information: American Youth Hostels, Dept. 855, PO Box 37613, Washington, DC 20013-7613; 202-783-6161.

CANADIAN HOSTELLING ASSOCIATION
Canada's hostelling program is similar to that of AYH, although it does not offer adventures designed exclusively for people over 50. Instead, it invites you to join

any of its adult trips (here, too, there is no maximum age limit), and hosts Elderhostel Canada programs at some of its more than 70 properties. In addition, as a member, you may lodge at a hostel for $4 to $14 per night, with meals from $2, in Canada—or at any other hostel in the world. Membership for one year costs $18. **For information:** Canadian Hostelling Association (L'Association canadienne de l'ajisme), 333 River Road, Vanier, Ontario K1L 8H9; 613-748-5638.

THE OVER THE HILL GANG

This is a club that welcomes fun-loving, adventurous, peppy people over 50 who are looking for action and contemporaries to pursue it with. No naps, no rockers, no sitting by the pool sipping planter's punch. The Over the Hill Gang started as a ski club many years ago but now is into lots of different activities, including travel (see Chapters 13 and 14 for more about the club). Most of the trips are sports-oriented, but some are just plain trips. For example, recent choices have included a Windjammer cruise in the Caribbean; ski trips to Vail, Colorado, Park City, Utah, and the Dolomites in Europe; white-water rafting trips down the Colorado; and a sight-seeing adventure in Switzerland.

You can join one of the many Gangs throughout the country or become a member at large and never lack for company and interesting places to go. Membership in a local Gang is $50 ($80 per couple). If there is no chapter in your area, you may join the national organization for $25 ($40 per couple) and participate in any of the activities.

For information: Over the Hill Gang, 13791 E. Rice Pl., Aurora, CO 80015; 303-699-6404.

OUTWARD BOUND USA

This organization, known for its wilderness-survival trips aimed at toughening up youngsters and young adults so they can gain self-confidence and self-esteem and learn to work as a team, has special short and popular courses for adults over 50. The physical activities are less strenuous, luckily, than they are for 16-year-olds, but you are expected to push yourself and the goal is the same—to help you discover that there are self-imposed limits, physical and mental, that you can go beyond. Some of the courses have the special goal of helping to effect a smooth transition from career to retirement.

The special four- to nine-day courses for people over 50 include sailing in the Florida Keys (January through June), sailing off the Maine coast (May or June), white-water rafting and hiking in North Carolina (May), canoeing in the lake country of Minnesota (summer), desert backpacking and rock climbing or white-water rafting on the West Coast (most of the year), and canoeing in the Florida Everglades (January through June).

On Outward Bound trips, you live in a tent or under a tarp, sleep in a sleeping bag, cook your own food. You must be in good health although you need not be a veteran athlete.

For information: Outward Bound USA, 384 Field Point Rd., Greenwich, CT 06830; 1-800-243-8520 (in Connecticut, 203-661-0797).

SENIOR TRAVEL EXCHANGE PROGRAM (STEP)

This is an idea borrowed from student-exchange programs and shares the same purpose of promoting goodwill and world peace, but it's strictly for adventurers over 50. STEP matches you up with foreign hosts in a choice of countries. You stay in their homes, pay nothing for bed and breakfast, but, in return, you'll play host for the same amount of time to overseas visitors who come to see your country.

Most of STEP's trips are for groups of people staying in different homes for four or five days in each of four communities and include sight-seeing and inland travel with a guide. But you may choose to stay in a home as a single traveler, as a couple, or with a small group of friends, with or without a prearranged itinerary.

STEP, operated by a California nonprofit organization, also offers vacations in low-cost resorts or inexpensive hotels, and, where there is no network of host homes, arranges bed-and-breakfast stays for minimal fees.

For information: Senior Travel Exchange Program, PO Box H, Santa Maria, California 93456; 805-925-5743.

GREAT NEW TRAVEL IDEAS

ALPINE AUTOTOUR

A novel program, this is for grown-up travelers in Europe who want independence and don't like the constant companionship and rigidity of an escorted bus trip but, at the same time, want the security of being part of a group. Translation: you get your own car, and you're free during the day, just as long as you turn up at your reserved first-class hotel in time for dinner with the rest of the group of independent adventurers.

On Autotour's three-week, five-country European tours, along with your car (you choose it), you get a daily map with a marked route of about 150 miles for the day. Drive at your own pace, stopping where you like, making whatever side detours you wish, and simply arrive at your day's destination by the appointed hour. The tours are spaced throughout the summer months, and one of them is specifically designated for people over 45.

For information: Alpine Autotour, 14 Forest Ave., Caldwell, NJ 07006; 1-800-433-7519 (in New Jersey, 201-226-9107); or your travel agent.

GRANDTRAVEL

GrandTravel is a new and innovative vacation program that offers trips for grandparents and their grandchildren so they can share the pleasures of traveling together. "It's a great way to strengthen the link between generations and create lasting memories for everyone," says Helena Koenig, the travel agent who started it. GrandTravel's series of itineraries, scheduled for normal school breaks, aims to appeal to both generations. It includes holiday tours to England; trips to Washington, DC, or Alaska; a tour through the American Southwest to learn about Indians; African safaris; a visit to the Galapagos Islands; a voyage to China and Japan; a stay in Israel; a tour of western national parks; and barge trips in Holland.

Actually, you don't have to be a grandparent to take the trips—aunts, uncles, cousins, godparents, and other surrogate grannies are welcome. Ranging from 7 to 17 days, the escorted tours include good hotels with recreation facilities, transportation by motorcoach with rest stops every two hours, and games, talks, and music on the buses. Each trip includes time for the older folks and the children to be alone with their own age group. The kids may go roller skating and dine on fried chicken—supervised, of course—while the grandparents do something grown up, such as going to a gourmet restaurant for dinner.

The arrangements for independent grandparent-grandchild vacations can also be planned by this agency.

For information: GrandTravel, The Ticket Counter, 6900 Wisconsin Ave., Chevy Chase, MD 20815; 1-800-247-7651 (in Maryland, 301-986-0790).

GRANDPARENT/GRANDCHILDREN HOLIDAYS

Saga Holidays offers another way for two generations to explore the world together. While you may be any age over 60 (your companion or spouse may be 50 or beyond), the kids must be from 6 to 16. Trips are planned for the Northwest, the national parks, the American Southwest, northwest national parks, and the California coast—and all during school vacation periods. See Chapter 7 for more about Saga's offerings.

For information: Saga Holidays, 120 Boylston St., Boston, MA 02116; 1-800-343-0273.

Chapter Four
Cutting Your Costs in Europe

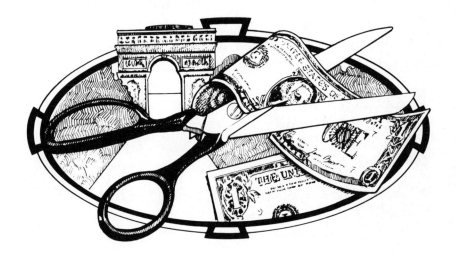

The most enthusiastic voyagers of all age groups, Americans over 50—one out of three adults and a quarter of the total population—spend more time and money on travel than anybody else, especially when it comes to going abroad. It's been estimated that more than 4 out of every 10 passport holders are at least 55 years old. And there's hardly a country in the world today that doesn't actively encourage mature travelers to come for a visit, because everybody has discovered that you are travel's "Now Generation."

Because you are currently being hotly pursued, you can take advantage of many good deals in other lands. This chapter gives you a rundown on ways to cut your European holiday costs, especially if you are planning your trip on your own.

But, first, keep in mind:

▶ Because this is a rapidly changing field as more and more nations and tourist attractions jump on the senior bandwagon, always check the rates as you go. You may find new bargains.
▶ Always have your necessary identification with you (your passport is an excellent ID) and don't be afraid to ask if your age qualifies you for a discount or special fare.

EUROPE BY RAIL

Here's a senior pass that can save you a bundle in Europe, *if* you qualify for it.

RAIL EUROP S

This wonderful little card is issued only to people who qualify as residents of a European country, which generally means you must live there for six months. If you plan an extended visit to Europe, you may be able to acquire one. Sometimes the residency rules are bent just a little. If so, you're in great luck. The card entitles you—if you're a woman of 60 or a man of 65—to 30 to 50 percent discounts on rail travel, first or second class, in 18 participating countries. Use it to travel within a country or across borders into others.

The participating nations include Austria, Belgium, Denmark, Finland, Greece, Hungary, Italy, Luxembourg, Norway, the Netherlands, Portugal, Republic of Ireland, Spain, Sweden, Switzerland, United Kingdom (including Northern Ireland), West Germany, and Yugoslavia.

Because the Rail Europ S pass is sold only in Europe and has no representative on this side of the ocean, you must wait until you get there to ferret out the details and see if your length of stay warrants it. It is available at major rail stations. The cost varies according to the country where you buy it, but in France, for example, where it must be used in conjunction with the Carte Vermeil, it costs 50 francs (about $7 at this writing).

EURAILPASS

And, of course, there is the well-known Eurailpass, valid for unlimited first-class train travel in 16 European countries (including Ireland but not Great Britain). There is no senior discount, but it's certainly worth buying if you plan to cover a lot of miles. Available for various numbers of days up to a month, the passes also get you free or reduced rates on many buses, ferries, and steamers. Traveling with a group of three or more people (or two or more in the off-season) and thereby qualifying for a Eurail Saverpass is especially cheap.

Make sure you buy your Eurailpass before leaving home.

For information: Call your travel agent or write Eurailpass, Box 10383, Stamford, CT 06904-2383

COUNTRY-BY-COUNTRY TRAVEL DEALS

AUSTRIA

Here a Railways Senior Citizen's ID may be purchased by women over 60 and men over 65 for about $15 at any major railroad station. It may be used to travel anywhere in Austria for half fare on the Austrian Federal Railways and its buses.

For information: Austrian National Tourist Office, 500 Fifth Ave., New York, NY 10036; 212-944-6880.

FRANCE

The Carte Vermeil (for women at 60 and men at 62) entitles you to purchase rail tickets within France for half price in either first or second class. Good for a year, it costs about $10 and can be bought at major railroad stations in France. In general, the 50 percent reduction applies from noon on Saturday until 3:00 P.M. on Sunday and from noon on Monday until 3:00 P.M. on

Friday. It is not valid on certain holidays, and you can't buy it in this country.

For information: French National Railroads, 610 Fifth Ave., New York, NY 10020; 212-582-2110.

GREAT BRITAIN

Here's where you're going to get your number-one best bargains in Europe, because the British are really into "the very good years," by which they generally mean over 60. There are discounts and special rates on almost everything—railroads, buses, airlines, canal cruises, many hotels, and just about every historical or tourist site.

A BritRail Senior Pass (for travelers 60 and over) gives you reduced rates on 8-day, 15-day, 22-day, and one-month passes for unlimited travel in England, Scotland, and Wales. It is valid in first class only. The rates are even better than for the regular BritRail Pass, which is a bargain for everyone else. It must be purchased through your travel agent *before* you leave our shores because it is not sold in Britain. By the way, the Eurailpass is not accepted in Great Britain.

In Northern Ireland, you can buy a Rail Runabout ticket at half price.

While people of other ages may need the Britexpress Card, you don't. The card costs $10 and is good for a one-third reduction on the network of routes throughout England, Scotland, and Wales on express buses operated by the National Express Bus Company and Scottish Citylink Coaches. You don't need it because you can automatically get a one-third reduction on any bus fare simply by showing your proof of age.

Be sure to buy an Open to View ticket—again before you leave home—because it gets you admission to more than 600 castles, palaces, and stately homes and gardens in the British Isles, including the Tower of London and Windsor Castle. It currently costs $29. And add to it an English Heritage Senior Citizen's Pass, available at the first English Heritage property you visit. This gives you free admission to many places and half-price admission to others.

Many theaters offer discounts, although sometimes only for matinees. Check at the box office or ask the hotel concierge.

Hotels often give senior discounts in the off-season (April through October), so always inquire when you make your reservations. The most notable are the Scottish Highland Hotels (1-800-223-1900 in the United States; 1-800-367-7441 in Canada), whose Golden Times rates for anybody over 60 are lower than the regular prices. You qualify if you stay a minimum of two nights. The Stakis Hotels in Scotland offer a break too. And Ladbroke Holidays' Good Companions program offers off-season week-long stays at a discount for those over 50. Others giving special rates to older guests are the Sheraton and Heritage hotels.

The last word: If you want to visit the Isle of Wight, check out Sealink's saver holidays for over-55s.

For information: The British Tourist Authority, 40 W. 57th St., New York, NY 10019; 212-581-4700. The Tourist Authority will also send you—if you request it—a free 96-page booklet called *Britain for the Very Good Years*.

GREECE

Here, if you are 60, male or female, you can buy a Hellenic Railways pass that's good for five free single train trips within Greece. When you've used up your five trips, you may travel on trains and buses at a 50 percent reduction. Valid for one year, the pass can be purchased at any major railroad station in Greece. The only hitch: there are some blackout periods when the card doesn't do the trick. These, of course, probably fall just when you don't want them to—from July 1 to the end of September, plus the 10 days before and after Easter and Christmas.

For information: The Greek National Tourist Organization, 645 Fifth Ave., New York, NY 10022; 212-421-5777.

MAKING FRIENDS BY MAIL

International Pen Friends is a pen-pal organization with more than 160,000 members all over the world. Anybody any age is eligible to join and be matched up with a pen friend in another country—an excellent way to make interesting contacts or practice a foreign language. Membership for one person aged 20 through 59 costs $14; for two people those ages, $20. For one person 60 or over, the membership fee is $10. You will receive a list of 14 names of people in a choice of countries and/or languages who are in your age range and share your interests. (Blind members may request cassette exchanges.)

For information: Send a self-addressed, stamped envelope to International Pen Friends, PO Box 290065, Brooklyn, NY 11229-0001.

ITALY

The Carta d'Argento (Silver Card), which costs about $4 and is valid for a year, entitles women at 62 and men at 65 to a 30 percent discount on Italian railways. It can be purchased at railroad stations in Italy at the special windows (Biglietti Speciali). Later, flash the card when you buy your tickets.

Note that if you are planning extensive train travel in Italy, however, you may wish to buy a travel-anywhere pass (available to tourists of all ages) called a BLTC, valid for unlimited travel for 8, 15, 21, or 30 days. It's cheap, and it may be a better buy for you. It must be purchased in the United States and is not available in Italy.

For information: Get a BLTC through your travel agent or from Italian State Railways, 666 Fifth Ave., New York, NY 10103; 212-397-2667.

LUXEMBOURG

Anybody over 65 gets half fare on trains and buses. Ask for the discount when you buy your tickets.

For information: The Luxembourg National Tourist Office, 801 Second Ave., New York, NY 10017; 212-370-9850.

THE NETHERLANDS

Holland has no special deals for people over 50, but it does offer two discount cards to everybody that are worth considering. One is the Holland Culture Card (about $15), which gives you free admission to more than 300 museums, art galleries, and studios; a 55 percent discount on a first-class Day Pass for unlimited travel by rail and bus; discounts on concerts and performances, sight-seeing tours, domestic flights, car rentals, etc. The other is the Holland Leisure Card (about $7.50), which provides substantial discounts on trains and buses, domestic air flights, car rentals, sight-seeing excursions, department-store purchases, entrance fees to many cultural attractions, etc. The cards may be purchased in the Netherlands or before you go.

For information: The Netherlands Board of Tourism, 355 Lexington Ave., New York, NY 10017; 212-370-7367.

SCANDINAVIAN COUNTRIES

If you are 65-plus, you can get around four Scandinavian countries—Denmark, Sweden, Norway, and Finland—by train more cheaply than other adults can.

Denmark gives you half fare outside of peak hours (peak hours are Fridays, 2:00 P.M. to 7:00 P.M.; Saturdays, 8:00 A.M. to noon; Sundays, 2:00 P.M. to midnight) and around the Christmas and Easter holidays.

The Swedish State Railways (SJ) give a 30 percent markdown in second class, with no restrictions on days or times. The discount also applies on the company's bus routes. Boats and ferries also offer special fares, depending on the season.

Norway's offer is 50 percent off the price of a first- or second-class ticket on any train, anytime. To get this, however, you must be 67.

Finland's Senior Citizen Card entitles you to 50 percent off on any train and 30 percent off any bus trip that's at least 47 miles one way—except during weekends and certain holidays.

Note that you should also look into the Scandinavian Bonus Pass. It is not age-oriented but gives discounts off the rates at more than 100 first-class hotels during the summer season in all of these countries plus Iceland.

For a small sum, you can pick up a city card in each capital—Copenhagen Card, Oslo Card, Helsinki Card, Stockholm Card (in Sweden the cards are also available for Gothenburg and Malmö). These cards can simplify your life in these metropolises by giving you unlimited travel on city transportation, free entry to museums and attractions, and discounts on sight-seeing tours, hotels, car rentals, restaurants, events.

For information: The Scandinavian National Tourist Offices, 655 Third Ave., New York, NY 10017; 212-949-2333.

SWITZERLAND

Switzerland offers some of the best discounts around. As part of its official Season for Seniors, the Swiss Hotel Association provides a list of hundreds of hotels that give reduced rates to women over 62 and men over 65 (if you're a couple, only one of you need be the required age). In most cases, however, you cannot get the discounts during peak holiday seasons, including midsummer.

Pick up a Swiss Railroads' Senior Half-Fare Travel card, which costs approximately $60 for a year and cuts fares in half for first or second class. Or you may prefer the 15-day Elite card, which has no age limitations and gives you half fare on all trains and buses for a 15-day period.

Note that there are two other discount cards available in Switzerland, not just to you but to everyone. One is the inexpensive Swiss Holiday Card that's recommended if you're doing a lot of traveling within the country. The card allows you unlimited travel on the entire network of the Swiss Federal Railways, including most private and mountain railroads, on lake steamers and most postal motorcoaches as well as public tramways and buses in the 24 largest Swiss cities, for varying periods of time, at a cost of less than $10 a day. It also lets you buy excursion tickets to mountaintops at 20 to 50 percent off.

The second is the Half-Fare Travel Card, which currently costs 100 Swiss francs (about $56) and is good for a year. Foreign visitors can purchase the half-fare card, valid for one month, for about $37. With the card, you can buy an unlimited number of transportation tickets of all varieties, including excursions to mountaintops, at half price.

For information: Consult your travel agent or the Swiss National Tourist Office in New York (608 Fifth Ave., New York, NY 10020; 212-757-5944) or San Francisco (250 Stockton St., San Francisco, CA 94108; 415-362-2260). In Switzerland, the transport cards are available at railroad stations and airports.

WEST GERMANY

German Rail offers the Senioren-Pass to women over 60 and men over 65, which gets you a 50 percent reduction on regular fares in first and second class. It's also good on some railroads in other countries if you start and finish your trip in Germany. Two varieties are available. Pass A costs about $30 for a year and is good only on Mondays, Tuesdays, Wednesdays, Thursdays, and Saturdays. Pass B, at about $50 a year, will do the job every day of the week.

Buy the senior pass at any main railroad station in Germany. You'll need your passport as proof of age.
For information: Germanrail, 747 Third Ave., New York, NY 10017; 212-308-3100.

Chapter Five
Trips and Tours for the Mature Traveler

A few sagacious over-50 organizations and travel agencies now cater to "the mature traveler." They choose destinations sure to appeal to those who have already seen much of the world, arrange trips that are leisurely and unhassled, give you like-minded contemporaries to travel with plus group hosts to smooth the way, and provide many services you've decided you're now entitled to. They also give you a choice between strenuous action-filled tours and those that are more relaxed. In fact, most of the agencies offer so many choices that the major problem becomes making a decision about where to go.

Options range from cruises in the Caribbean or the Greek Isles to grand tours of the Orient, sight-seeing excursions in the United States, trips to the Canadian Rockies, theater tours of London, African safaris and snorkeling vacations on the Great Barrier Reef off Australia. There's no place in the world over-50s won't go.

Among the newer and most popular trends are apartment-hotel complexes in American and European resort areas, as well as apartments in major cities. Here you can stay put for as long as you like, using the apartment as a home base for short-range roaming and exploring.

To qualify for most of the trips, one member of the party is supposed to meet the minimum age requirement, and the rest may be younger.

THE OVER-50 CLUBS

AARP TRAVEL SERVICE
AARP (The American Association of Retired Persons) is a huge club (see Chapter 20) that offers all kinds of

wonderful benefits, including myriad trips and tours and discounted cruises, all planned with 50-plus voyagers in mind.

Every season, members get to choose from scores of travel possibilities at enticingly good group rates. There are fully escorted motorcoach tours, deluxe or budget, to Europe, the Soviet Union, Hawaii, Mexico, China, the South Pacific, the United States, and Canada. There are Hosted Holidays in Europe, Mexico, or the Orient, where you will live in an apartment or a hotel, using it as a home base, and exploring the area with the guidance of a local AARP host. Other AARP options include trips to regional celebrations (such as the Mardi Gras in New Orleans) and "independent travel," where you choose lodgings from a selection of AARP-approved properties.

AARP's cruise vacations provide a wide variety of cruise lines with trips to many exotic places, all at substantial savings over regular rates.

If you're a member of AARP, you have already been sent a pile of material about its Travel Service. And you receive its magazine, *Modern Maturity*, which provides ongoing information about the trips and how to sign up for them.

For information: AARP Travel Service, 5855 Green Valley Circle, Culver City, CA 90230; 1-800-227-7737 from 9:00 A.M. to 5:00 P.M. your time.

MATURE OUTLOOK TRAVEL BENEFIT

Mature Outlook, the over-50 club that's run by Sears (see Chapter 20), also offers great travel advantages and benefits to its members. If you join, you can see the world on its guided tours and cruises that will take you anyplace from China to the South Pacific to a safari in Africa or a cruise through the Panama Canal or up the Alaskan coast. There are even a Tahiti cruise and a shopping tour of port cities in the Far East—Hong Kong, Bangkok, Singapore, and Beijing. All of the trips will cost you considerably less than the going regular prices because you will benefit from group rates.

All of Mature Outlook's tours have escorts or special local representatives to ease your way and organize activities. If you are traveling alone, you may ask for the names and telephone numbers of others in the group who are looking for roommates so you may choose your own, or you may ask to be assigned one. If you request a roommate and none is forthcoming, you will pay only half of the regular single supplement fee.

For information: Mature Outlook, PO Box 1205, Glenview, IL 60025; 1-800-262-0123.

TRAVEL AGENCIES THAT CATER TO OVER-50s

SAGA HOLIDAYS

This 35-year-old British travel firm (in England, people have been known to joke that Saga stands for "Send a Granny Away") specializes in travel for people over 60 (and their spouses or friends over 50). It opened up in the United States and Australia just a few years ago and is probably now the largest travel company in this field. On its trips, which may be booked only by direct mail or telephone and not through travel agents, Americans find fellow travelers from Great Britain, Australia, and other English-speaking nations. The mix of people from different cultures is an added attraction for many voyagers.

Once your name is on Saga's mailing list, you will be faced with constant temptation as the enticing brochures keep on coming. Saga's special features include all-inclusive prices from many departure cities, tour escorts or local guides on call, flight insurance, special Singles Holidays (see Chapter 6) that give you an opportunity to travel with other people who aren't half of a couple, roommate matchups if you want them or, if no roommate is available, only half price on the single supplement.

And more: Grandparents/Grandchildren Holidays (see Chapter 3), free travel if you can gather 20 friends to go on the same trip, a free Travel Med+Card so you can carry your own medical record data with you on a microfilm chip, and refunds if you must cancel your trip for medical reasons.

The Saga Holidays Club ($5 for three years) gives some good benefits including a quarterly newsletter, a yearly jamboree, social gatherings, and a list of Penfriends and Partnerships so you can meet people through the mail, perhaps finding a perfect traveling companion if you are on your own. This outfit's thought of it all!

It also offers extended stays in apartments or hotels abroad and Add-On Holidays whereby you can tack one trip onto another once you are overseas.

For information: Saga Holidays, 120 Boylston St., Boston, MA 02116; 1-800-366-SAGA from 8:00 A.M. to 8:00 P.M. EST during the week and 8:00 A.M. to 5:00 P.M. EST on Saturdays.

GRAND CIRCLE TRAVEL

Grand Circle caters to people over 50, but if you're a little younger and you really want to go on one of its trips, that's okay too. Founded 30 years ago, this tour operator was the first U.S. company to market senior travel and has escorted approximately half a million Americans all over the world.

Grand Circle's trips will take you everywhere, even on an Around the World Tour that stops in "17 exotic destinations" from Katmandu to Nairobi to Beijing. In addition to an endless choice of traditional escorted tours and cruises, this company—which books tours only by mail or telephone—has other intriguing features. For example, it operates a number of apartments and residential hotels in the United States and the rest of the world, dubbed the Extended Vacations program for travelers over 50. Your apartment or hotel provides a home base—in such places as London, Hawaii, Italy, Hong Kong, Costa del Sol, Yugoslavia, Portugal, Australia, Fiji Islands, Switzerland—for anywhere from 2 to 25 weeks. This way, you can explore at your leisure and perhaps add optional excursions to nearby vacation spots.

And there are other Grand Circle programs. The Countryside Tours let you stay in destinations that aren't very well known, and Tour/Extended trips combine tours with one-week stayovers wherever you like.

As for single travelers, GCT offers special departure dates with a 50 percent discount on the standard hotel and apartment single supplements and will help you find a travel roommate of the same sex and interests if you want one. If one isn't readily at hand, you will be charged only half the single supplement. (See Chapter 6.)

GCT's Travel Club ($5 for three years) gives you a quarterly magazine (with a Pen Pal section), plus special trips and discounts for members only.

For information: Grand Circle Travel, 347 Congress St., Boston, MA 02210; 1-800-248-3737 (in Massachusetts, 1-800-535-8333) Monday through Friday, 8:00 A.M. to 7:00 P.M. EST and Saturday 9:00 A.M. to 5:00 P.M. EST.

GOLDEN AGE TRAVELLERS

This over-50 club specializes in cruises, although it offers other trips as well. When you join the club for $7 a year ($10 per couple), you receive a monthly newsletter with a listing of upcoming adventures, discounts, and bonuses on major cruise lines. Other inducements are tour escorts on every venture and a credit of $15 to $25 per person against the transportation costs to the airport on certain trips. Single travelers may choose to be enrolled in the "Roommates Wanted" list to help find a companion to share the costs.

For members in the San Francisco area, where GAT is located, there are monthly meetings where you may meet fellow travelers and learn about upcoming trips, limousine service to and from the airport or pier, and one-day mini-tours.

Most of this agency's trips are cruises but cruises everywhere in the world—including the Caribbean, Alaska, the Mediterranean, China and Japan, the South Pacific, between Montreal and New York, and down the Mexican coast and through the Panama

Canal and on up the Atlantic coast to Philadelphia. There is also a selection of land tours.

For information: Golden Age Travellers, 1520 Union Street, San Francisco, CA 94123; 1-800-652-1683 in California, 1-800-258-8880 elsewhere in the United States.

MORE, MORE, MORE

BREEZE TOURS

Mature travelers are Breeze's specialty, with no-hassle escorted sight-seeing trips to Hawaii, Australia and New Zealand (with optional extensions to Fiji, Tahiti, or Hawaii), and England. In Hawaii, you may choose to make "independent arrangements," which means you settle into a hotel or condominium and do your own wandering in a rental car with unlimited mileage. Another way to do it is to choose the Golfing in Paradise trip, which takes you and your set of clubs to some of the top golf courses in the Hawaiian Islands.

A popular trip is the all-inclusive one-week tour of British stately homes and castles, with departure dates from May through September. Several of the weeks are reserved for groups of "mature singles," something to keep in mind if that's what you are.

For information: Call your travel agent or contact Breeze Tours, 2750 Stickney Point Rd., Sarasota, FL 33581; 1-800-237-5630 (in Florida, 1-800-282-5630).

MAYFLOWER TOURS

Mayflower plans trips for people "55 or better." Most departures are from Chicago with overnight accommodations arranged for travelers from surrounding states. Some of the agency's more far-flung tours, however, leave from other cities. All trips are fully escorted by tour directors whose job it is to make sure all goes well and everybody has fun. The pace is leisurely, and rest stops are scheduled for every couple of hours. You travel by air-conditioned motorcoach, stay in quality hotels or motels, and eat most of your meals together.

If you are a single traveler and make your trip reservation at least 30 days before departure, you'll get a roommate or travel at the regular double rate. And if you live in the Chicago area, you can join the Serendipity Club, a social club for singles, to help you find your own travel companion to share a room and costs.

All of the agency's trips are within the United States (Hawaii included), with tours, for example, through the Canadian Rockies, the Pennsylvania Dutch country, or Georgia's Golden Isles.

For information: Call your travel agent or contact Mayflower Tours, 1225 Warren Ave., Downers Grove, IL 60515; 1-800-323-7604 or 312-960-3430.

PLEASANT HAWAIIAN HOLIDAYS

As you may have guessed, this company takes you to the Hawaiian Islands. Its trips are designed for people 60 and upward, and the rates apply to anybody sharing the room. Its holiday trips, from 3 to 15 nights, provide flights, hotels, breakfast, often a rental car, transfers, special on-location counselors, a lei around your neck when you arrive, and a "full-color Memory Album" when you leave. Most trips include a combination of islands and give you a list of hotels and condominiums from which to choose your lodgings.

For information: Call your travel agent or contact Pleasant Hawaiian Holidays, 2404 Townsgate Rd., Westlake Village, CA 91361; 1-800-242-9244.

CHOOSING A PLACE TO SETTLE DOWN

Retirement Explorations conducts group 11- to 15-day tours to several parts of the world that it considers to be "ideal retirement communities." You'll tour areas of Costa Rica, or southern Portugal and Spain's Costa del Sol, or the Guadalajara area of Mexico, and attend a series of seminars and meetings with local authorities in the medical, legal, business, investment, and real-estate fields. You'll have conversations and meals with Americans already living there as well as sightseeing adventures. In this way, says Jane Parker, a retirement planning counselor who runs this tour agency, you can find out first-hand what it's like to live in these foreign lands before you make any hard decisions. All of these places were chosen and rated according to cost of living, taxes, health care, climate, safety, friendliness of the people, government stability, and cultural opportunities.

For information: Retirement Explorations, 19414 Vineyard Lane, Saratoga, CA 95070; 408-257-5378.

SENIOR ESCORTED TOURS

Specializing in vacations in Cape May, a beautiful little coastal town at the southern tip of New Jersey that abounds in Victoriana, this company also offers package trips to such places as Orlando, Florida; Nashville and Gatlinburg, Tennessee; Cape Cod, Massachusetts; and the Catskills in New York—most of them including all meals. There are cruises down the Mississippi River, along the coast of Alaska, and through the Panama Canal, as well as adventures in Australia and the U.S. national parks.

For information: Call your travel agent or contact Senior Escorted Tours, 223 N. Main St., Cape May Court House, NJ 08210; 1-800-222-1254 (in New Jersey, 1-800-222-1257).

SWISSAIR'S GOLDEN AGE TOURS

Switzerland's airline offers special two-week group vacations for older travelers. You can go with a club or an organization or form your own group of 20 or more friends. The trips can be tailored to your own tastes, but, in general, you will spend a week each in Lucerne and Montreux or a week each in Lugano and Interlaken or two weeks in Lucerne. And an optional week in Zurich may be added. There are plenty of day trips if you want them and time to stroll around on your own, but staying put in one hotel for a week or more simplifies your life—no need to pack and unpack every day.

For information: Call your travel agent or Swissair at 1-800-221-4750.

TRAFALGAR'S AUTUMN YEARS TOURS

Trafalgar's, a British travel agency, offers "escorted motorcoach tours for the over-55s," taking clients on

European trips, combining city sights with scenery. A couple of the possibilities here are 21 days in England, Wales, Ireland, and Scotland, or 29 days moseying all the way from England through Belgium, Holland, Germany, Switzerland, Austria, to Italy and France.

Along with tourists from all of the British Commonwealth countries (about a third of the travelers come from Australia, a quarter from the United States, and the rest from South Africa, Hong Kong, Canada, England, or New Zealand), you are escorted and entertained by professional British tour directors, stay in first-class hotels, and move at a relaxed pace.

For information: Call your travel agent or contact Trafalgar Tours, 21 E. 26th Street, New York, NY 10010; 1-800-854-0103 or 212-689-8977.

TWA'S GETAWAY CLUB 60

TWA has designed many vacation trips specifically for people over 60 (and their companions of any age), including escorted tours in Europe, luxury cruises, a month-long Grand Europe tour, eight-day tours of America, and island holidays in the Bahamas, Caribbean, and Hawaii. All of them are unhurried and relaxed. Prices are good because of the group rates.

Among Getaway Club 60's bonuses are free travel insurance, no-fee traveler's checks, a free credit card, a subscription to the *Senior Travel Newsletter*, and shopping discounts. Every trip has its own tour director and includes most meals.

Though this is called a club, there is no membership fee—you become a member when you book a trip.

For information: Call your travel agent or TWA at 1-800-GETAWAY.

RETIRING IN MEXICO

Retire in Mexico (RIM), a travel company based in California, has organized a series of seminars and educational tours for people who are thinking about the possibility of retiring in Mexico, a neighboring country where the American dollar currently goes very far. Could Mexico provide a happy home for you? You can find out by attending seminars given periodically in West Coast cities and New York, and then, if the idea intrigues you, signing on for a group visit to one or more of about a dozen south-of-the-border areas. You travel around the town and countryside by car or van with a small number of other potential retirees, and attend lectures on such subjects as health facilities, housing, investments, Mexican culture, and immigration.

On a typical tour, for example, you would spend three nights in Mexico City, then two each in San Miguel de Allende, Guanajuato, Morelia, and three in Guadalajara. There are other choices as well, all places with significant North American populations. In each area, you get conferences and tours conducted in English. (Point of information: Mexicana Airlines gives 10 to 20 percent discounts, depending on the season, to travelers over 65 and their any-age companions on flights to Mexico from 11 U.S. gateway cities. See Chapter 7.)

For information: Barvi Tours, 11658 Gateway Blvd, Los Angeles, CA 90064; 1-800-824-7102 (in California, 213-475-1861).

YUGOTOURS

It may not come as a surprise that Yugotours, owned by the Yugoslavian government, features trips to Yugoslavia. It has become known for its "Prime of Your Life Vacations" for anybody over 50 (plus companions of any age). Offered all year round, the vacations take you via Yugoslav Airlines to your pick of resorts in Yugoslavia on the coast, at inland lakes, or in the mountains, depending upon the season. Rates vary according to the time of year but are all-inclusive and very reasonable.

On this venture, you can customize your trip to suit yourself, taking it slow or becoming involved in the activities organized by the tour director in your hotel. You may spend your entire vacation in one resort, or in a combination of places, and you may stay as many weeks as you like. Included in the package are breakfast and dinner.

While you're there, you may avail yourself of special mini-holidays—three nights in a choice of cities in nearby countries, such as Rome, Athens, Budapest, Istanbul, or Prague. And, at the end of your stay, you have the option of prolonging your trip with special extensions, like a week in the Soviet Union, a tour of the Dalmatian Coast, or a cruise on the Adriatic Sea.

For information: Call your travel agent or contact Yugotours, 350 Fifth Ave., New York, NY 10118; 1-800-223-5298 (in New York State, 212-563-2400).

CRUISING THE HIGH SEAS

Cruises have always appealed to the mature crowd. In fact, most sailings abound with people who are at least a decade or two out of college. So, whatever trip you choose, you are sure to find suitable companionship. However, there are some special deals designed especially for you.

BERMUDA STAR LINE

For example, this line, whose ships now ply the waters

between Florida and Mexico much of the year, gives anybody 60 years old or beyond (and cabinmates) a 10 percent discount on many of its sailings. Included are the *SS Bermuda Star*'s 7-day cruises from San Diego to the Mexican Riviera and its 18-day cruises from Los Angeles and San Diego down the west coast of Mexico, through the Panama Canal to Cartagena, Colombia; Cozumel, Mexico; and New Orleans. The 10 percent discount also applies to selected sailings of the line's *SS Canada Star* and the *SS Veracruz*. And, if you want to go as a group of mature travelers, you'll get an even better break.

For information: Call your travel agent or Bermuda Star Line at 1-800-237-5361.

PREMIER CRUISE LINES

Combine four-night cruises to the Bahamas out of Port Canaveral, Florida with three days in Disney World, and, if you are over 59, get a 10 percent discount. Anybody else who shares your cabin gets the discount, too. Although the savings can't be combined with other promotional rates, it can be added to the advantages you earn by booking early (upgrades in cabin category).

Here's what you get: A four-night cruise to Nassau and Salt Cay in the Bahamas, then three nights in a hotel near Disney World, free admission to Disney's Magic Kingdom and Epcot Center, as well as Spaceport, USA, plus a rental car with unlimited mileage thrown in.

For information: Call your travel agent, or contact Premier Cruise Lines, P.O. Box 573, Cape Canaveral, FL 32920; 1-800-327-7113 (in Florida, 305-783-5061).

SENIOR-WORLD

Senior-World caters to people over 45 who like to cruise the seas and spend time ashore sight-seeing, shopping, and sunning. Using major cruise lines and charging fares that are usually well below the regular tariffs, Senior-World schedules its trips at nonpeak times—commonly in fall and early winter. At this moment, destinations include Caribbean ports as well as Cancun and Cozumel in Mexico. Coming up: cruises to the Far East.

Cruise passengers are guaranteed lower berths, the first sitting in the dining room, exclusive shore excursions, and special activities such as cocktail parties just for your crowd.

A special escort is sent along on every cruise to organize shipboard activities and shore excursions and, in general, to make sure all goes well.

Accommodations for solo travelers are arranged on a shared basis, meaning that you'll be assigned a suitable roommate if you haven't brought your own.

For information: Call your travel agent or contact Senior-World, Gramercy Travel, 444 Madison Ave., New York, NY 10022; 1-800-223-6490.

SOUTH FLORIDA CRUISES

This cruise clearinghouse specializes in bargain trips to the Caribbean, Mexico, South America, the Panama Canal, Europe, Alaska, the South Pacific, and the Far East, giving passengers substantially reduced rates. Its method is to purchase large blocks of space on brand-name cruise lines and pass some of the savings along. What's more, it has declared it will give you an

additional discount of about $50 per cabin if you are over 50 years of age and mention the "Unbelievably Good Deals and Great Adventures Special." In other words, say you found this information in this book!
For information: South Florida Cruises, Inc., 2005 Cypress Creek Rd., Fort Lauderdale, FL 33309; 1-800-327-SHIP (in Florida, 305-493-6300).

SPECIAL TRIPS TO ISRAEL

Israel is a favorite travel destination for many over-50 travelers, so several tour operators and Jewish organizations have designed visits especially for them. The trips are usually at least three weeks long and organized in a leisurely fashion with plenty of free time.

AMERICAN JEWISH CONGRESS
The AJC runs lots of trips everywhere, but especially to Israel, and has one tour oriented toward people with plenty of time for an easygoing itinerary. Called Israel Leisurely, it lasts 27 days. You'll stay 6 nights in Tel Aviv, 10 nights in Jerusalem, with shorter stays in other areas. Included are breakfasts and dinners, a cruise on the Sea of Galilee, an archaeological seminar, a musical show, and a few other special events. Lots of time on your own too.

If you're traveling alone, you may want to choose AJC's once-a-year late-summer Israel Fortnight for singles over 55.
For information: American Jewish Congress, 15 E. 84th St., New York, NY 10028; 1-800-221-4694.

EL AL

The Israeli airline, which packages trips, has planned its 22-day Israel at Leisure Tour for over-50s, with 6 nights in Tel Aviv, 12 nights in Jerusalem, and 2 in the Galilee, all with an English-speaking guide.

El Al's new Jewish Heritage Tours—one to eastern Europe (Poland or Czechoslovakia/Hungary) and another to Poland only, before flying to Israel—are meant to give American Jews an opportunity to explore their roots and are planned with older travelers in mind.

For information: Call your travel agent or contact El Al, 850 Third Ave., New York, NY 10022; 1-800-352-5786 (in New York, 212-940-0600).

NATIONAL COUNCIL OF YOUNG ISRAEL

Once a year, the Senior League of this organization offers a three-week tour of the country, a package deal that includes everything.

For information: National Council of Young Israel, 3 W. 16th St., New York, NY 10011; 212-929-1525.

ZOA RETIREES PROGRAM

See Chapter 19 for information on this voluntary work program.

Chapter Six
Singles on the Road

MATCHMAKERS

Lots of over-50s love to travel but haven't got a handy companion to do it with. No need to give up your dreams of faraway places if you don't want to go it alone, because there are many organizations and even travel packagers ready to come to your aid. Some offer special trips for mature singles where you meet and mingle with others on the loose. And many help match you up with a fellow traveler who is also seeking a compatible person with whom to hit the road or share a room and expenses.

TRAVEL COMPANION EXCHANGE

Specializing in finding the right travel companion for all age groups "from 18 to 85," TCE matches up single, divorced, or widowed travelers for joint adventures. Run by travel expert Jens Jurgen, who is always dreaming up new ways to matchmake, this organization really works at making happy connections and has been very successful. Its periodic newsletters are stuffed with listings of members describing themselves, their preferences, and their special interests. For more details, you send for their Profile Pages—or others send for yours—with addresses and telephone numbers so you may judge compatibility for yourself. **For information:** Travel Companion Exchange Inc., Box 833, Amityville, NY 11701; 516-454-0880.

LONERS ON WHEELS

Most of the members of Loners on Wheels, a 54-chapter national recreational club, are retired and over 50, but the only ironclad rule for membership is that you be single! "There are literally hundreds of campouts each year sponsored by the chapters, as well as about 12 large rallies each year in various parts of the country and Canada," according to its literature. All kinds of RVs are included, as well as all kinds of people who participate in all kinds of recreational and educational activities. Aside from the outings, there are Loners on Wheels campgrounds in the Ozarks, Florida, and California.

For information: Write to Loners on Wheels, 808 Lester St., Poplar Bluff, MO 63901.

PARTNERS-IN-TRAVEL

This group is devoted to making travel a happier experience for solo travelers through contacts and connections. Via a newsletter and its Match Up service, its goal is to link up travel companions, most of them what you might call "mature" and most of them Californians, although some members live in other states. Again, the newsletter prints mini-listings that will be followed up by more detailed profiles if you request them.

An additional service is a Vacation-Home Exchange program available to members who wish to extend hospitality and/or accommodations to fellow members.

For information: Partners-in-Travel, PO Box 491145, Los Angeles, CA 90049; 213-476-4869.

TRAVEL MATES

This group devotes its energies to helping you get together with compatible traveling companions. After you join, complete a questionnaire, and request a "search," you will be sent background information on up to five prospective travel partners in your vicinity whose interests and personalities seem to match yours. You take it from there. Your annual $15 membership fee includes your first search; after that, additional matching costs $5 each. There is no age minimum, but most members are over 50.

For information: Travel Mates, 49 W. 44th St., New York, NY 10036; 212-221-6565.

TOUR PACKAGERS

Several tour operators who specialize in escorted trips for people in their prime try to find roommates (of the same sex) to share your room or cabin so you can avoid paying the single supplement. And, if they can't manage to find a suitable roommate, they will usually reduce the supplement even though you'll have your own private room. Some run singles trips as well. In any case, keep in mind that you'll hardly have time or opportunity to be lonely on the typical escorted tour run by these agencies. If you are planning an extended stay in one place, however, you may have more need for company.

For more about the tour operators listed below, see Chapter 5. Other companies may offer the same singles-matching service, though they don't make a point of it, so always ask about it if you're interested.

BREEZE TOURS
Catering to mature travelers, Breeze Tours reserves some of its summertime one-week tours of British stately homes and castles for groups of singles.

For information: Breeze Tours, 2750 Stickney Point Rd., Sarasota, FL 33581; 1-800-237-5630.

GOLDEN AGE TRAVELLERS

An over-50 club, Golden Age Travellers will enroll you in its "Roommates Wanted" list if you wish help in finding a companion with whom to share the costs and the fun.

For information: Golden Age Travellers, 1520 Union St., San Francisco, CA 94123; 1-800-258-8880 (in California, 1-800-652-1683).

GRAND CIRCLE TRAVEL

Another tour operator that tries to match singles with appropriate roommates if they request them. If there are none at hand, you will be charged only half the single supplement for your own room. This company also offers special singles departure dates, with 50 percent off the standard hotel and apartment single supplements. Plus, its newsletter has a Pen Pal section that allows members of GCT's Travel Club to make new friends and perhaps find people to travel with.

For information: Grand Circle Travel, 347 Congress St., Boston, MA 02210; 1-800-248-3737 (in Massachusetts, 1-800-535-8333).

MAYFLOWER TOURS

Another travel operator with mature travelers as its focus, Mayflower also gets you a roommate or, if that's not possible, charges you only the regular double rate without the single supplement. Its Serendipity Club in Chicago provides an additional way to match yourself up with a potential traveling companion.

For information: Mayflower Tours, 1225 Warren Ave., Downers Grove, IL 60515; 1-800-323-7604 or 312-960-3430.

SAGA HOLIDAYS

A tour company specializing in trips for people over 60 (see Chapter 5), Saga Holidays will try to find a roommate for you on its escorted tours. If there is none to be found, you will be charged only half the single supplement. Its Penfriends and Partnerships program, part of the Saga Holiday Club, prints "personals" in its newsletter so members may meet each other by mail and perhaps find a travel partner in the bargain. This company also schedules several exclusive Singles Departures, usually to destinations within the United States, each season. On these, the single supplement prices are reduced and you are guaranteed a roommate if you want one, or you will get your own room at the twin-share price.

For information: Saga Holidays, 120 Boylston St., Boston, MA 02116; 1-800-366-SAGA.

SENIOR-WORLD

Senior-World specializes in cruises and will provide a cabinmate for you if you want one. Be sure to specify your desires when you book.

For information: Senior-World, Gramercy Travel, 444 Madison Ave., New York, NY 10022; 1-800-223-6490.

SUDDENLY SINGLE TOURS

Trips for mature singles—to China, Portugal and Spain, Israel and Egypt, or Russia, for example—and special cruises as well—are this group's specialty. If you sign up, you will be in the company of a whole bunch of people in the same situation because this out-fit caters to people who have suddenly become single in midlife. Its travel programs "are designed with your maturity, tastes, and needs in mind."

For information: Suddenly Single Tours, Ltd., 161 Dreiser Loop, New York, NY 10475; 212-379-8800.

Chapter Seven
Airfares:
Improving with Age

One thing that improves with age (yours) is airfare. Almost every airline in existence now offers discounted senior fares and sometimes they are the best deals around. The airlines are currently using four ways of attracting mellow travelers: clubs with discounts, discounts without clubs, unlimited-mileage passes, and coupon books. That's because we have proved to be the hottest travel market to tap today. We are a vast and growing group of careful consumers with money in our pockets and time on our hands during slack off-peak periods, just when the airlines like to fill up seats.

The minimum age for senior fares is 60. Most programs allow a companion of any age, regardless of sex or relationship, to travel with you at the same reduced fare, although occasionally that person must pay a fee for the privilege. In some cases, however, your younger companion must be married to you to get the slashed prices.

Several airlines have arrangements with car-rental companies and hotel chains to provide discounts on these, too. (See Chapter 8 for more on car rentals and Chapter 10 for more on hotels and motels.)

But, first, keep in mind:

▶ Always ask your travel agent or the airline reservations clerk to get you the *lowest possible fare*. Mention the fact that you qualify for a senior discount, but be prepared to jump ship if you can get a better deal by going with a special promotional rate or a super supersaver fare—although sometimes your discount can cut these lowest fares even lower.
▶ Keep in mind that the restrictions you must fly by may not be worth the savings. Always examine the

fees and conditions and decide whether you can live with them. There may be blackout periods around major holidays when you can't use your discount, departures only on certain days or hours, restrictions on the season of the year, or stiff penalties for flight changes. In some plans, you must travel the entire distance on one airline even if connections are poor. It's not easy to sort out the offers because some carriers give better discounts but more hassles—or vice versa—so make comparisons before arriving at a decision.

▶ Before you decide to buy a yearly pass or a coupon book, figure out how many trips you're likely to make during the next year. Unless you see clear savings, you are better off with individual tickets. But if you travel frequently, or would do so once you had the pass, then it could be an excellent buy.

▶ Book your flights as early as possible for the best fares and the most available seats (frequently, the number of seats is severely limited). Try to couple your senior discounts with ultimate supersaver fares, which require 30-day advance purchase and include other restrictions on length of stay, and days on which you may fly.

▶ Be prepared to present a membership card (if you are flying as a member of a club) and a valid proof of age at the check-in counter. It's possible that your discount will not be honored if you don't have that proof with you, and you will have to pay the difference.

Now for some of the potential bargain offers. Be advised that airfares and airline policies often change overnight, so call the airline that interests you for an update.

U.S. SKIES: MAJOR AIRLINES

AMERICAN AIRLINES

The American Airlines Senior SAAvers Club entitles anyone over 65 to a 10 percent discount off all fares, even the lowest, without restrictions on times, days, or seasons, to destinations in the continental United States, Hawaii, Mexico, Canada, and Germany. There is no limit on how many trips you may make.

Lifetime membership costs $25. If you choose a membership with a companion option (for an additional one-time fee of $75), you may travel with a person of any age, who may vary from trip to trip and who gets the same 10 percent reduction.

Membership also gets you discounts on car rentals, hotels, and travel packages, as well as automatic enrollment in the frequent-flyer program. A club newsletter keeps you up to date.

For information: Call your travel agent or 1-800-433-7300.

BRANIFF

Braniff's Senior Citizen Discount gives you 15 percent off any fare, even the lowest 30-day advance-purchase fare. It also gives the same discount to a traveling companion, no matter what age. All you have to do is state that you want the senior discount when you make your reservation. There are no restrictions, no blackouts during peak holiday periods, and no club fee.

For information: Call your travel agent or 1-800-BRANIFF.

CONTINENTAL

You can get a senior citizen fare, simply by asking for it, in many areas where Continental flies when you purchase a regular coach seat. The amount of the reduction varies from place to place. But, before you take it, always check first to see if this gives you the *lowest possible available fare* because sometimes the max fare will be even lower than this special discount provides.

And then there's Continental's Golden Travelers Club, open to anyone over 65. This gives you a 10 percent discount off *any* fare (which means it will be applied *on top of* any promotional fare, including the senior citizen fare) on all flights within mainland United States and Mexico. Be sure you get everything that's coming to you—get your lowest fare, senior or not, and then take another 10 percent off that.

A companion of any age who accompanies you on the same flight—and may differ from trip to trip—will also get 10 percent off. Lifetime membership in the club costs $25; membership with companion privileges costs $100.

As a member, you get substantial discounts at two hotel chains and two car-rental agencies, as well as frequent-flyer mileage credits.

For information: Call your travel agent or 1-800-525-0280.

DELTA

Delta Senior Citizen Discount Tickets are sold to travelers over 62 and currently cost $368 ($92 each trip) for four tickets or $616 ($77 per trip) for eight tickets. Nontransferable and nonrefundable, the tickets may be used for a year, except during the Christmas–New Year holiday period, on flights to any Delta destination in the United States and Puerto Rico except Hawaii. Reservations are accepted only within six days of departure, and travel is limited to Tuesday, Wednesday, Thursday, and Saturday. Frequent-flyer credits are yours when you fly with the coupons which may be purchased the very day you are flying.

For information: Call your travel agent or Delta at 1-800-221-1212.

EASTERN

Eastern was the first airline to target the lucrative senior travel market, and its Seniority System now offers three different choices.

The first is its Get-Up-and-Go Passport, a good buy for people over 62 who plan a lot of trips. For the current price of $1,299, you get virtually unlimited travel for a year to more than 100 destinations in the United States, Canada, and Puerto Rico. You may buy a second pass for a younger traveling companion at the same price. The airline guarantees that if you don't use at least $999 worth of travel over a year, you will get a refund. Other options: For $1,499, you may fly throughout the United States and the Caribbean, too. For $1,799, you may fly first class. All deals include discounts on car rentals and rooms at several hotel chains.

Among the restrictions: You may fly only from noon Monday through noon Thursday and all day Saturday. There are blackout periods during major holidays. Seats may be limited. You are entitled to no more than three one-way trips, in the same direction, from any one city to any other single city during that year.

Eastern's second plan is its Senior Discount Coupons, again for those 62 and up. This provides you with four one-way trips to anywhere the airline flies in the United States and Puerto Rico for $368 ($92 per trip), or eight one-way trips for $618 ($77.25 per trip). Again, seats are limited and you may travel only from noon Monday through noon Thursday and all day Saturday.

The third option is the Senior Discount Card, for which you must be 65. With the card, you may travel at any available fare, anytime, anywhere, with a 10 percent discount. This means you have as good a chance as anyone else of getting on the flights you want, even at holiday time.

On all of Eastern's plans, you will get frequent-flyer credits for the mileage you've flown.

For information: Call your travel agent or 1-800-EASTERN.

PAN AMERICAN

This airline charges you only $45 on its shuttles from New York to Washington or Boston if you are over 65 (the regular price as this book goes to press is $89; $69 on Saturdays and on Sundays until 2:30 P.M). You may fly only at these hours, however: 10:30 A.M. to 2:30 P.M. and 7:30 P.M. to 9:30 P.M., Monday through Friday; all day Saturday; and until 2:30 P.M. on Sunday. You are guaranteed a seat—simply show up, with proof of age, half an hour before flight time. Frequent-flyer credits apply.

For information: Call 1-800-221-1111.

PIEDMONT

One of two varieties of senior savings on Piedmont is its Senior Class Travel Club. You may join at age 60 for $25 for a lifetime membership, plus $75 for a companion membership. Once you've hit your 65th birthday, you will be given a 10 percent discount on any fare in the continental United States and Canada. Your companion of any age, who may differ from trip to trip, gets the same reduced fare.

Before 65, you may cash in on the other privileges of the club, which include discounts on rooms at Radisson and Stouffer hotels, car rentals, vacation packages, and cruises. You get a newsletter to keep you up to date on new offers. You are automatically enrolled in the frequent-flyer program and receive double mileage credits for every trip you take.

Piedmont's Senior Discount Coupons, the other choice, give you, at age 62, four one-way tickets good for any destination within the continental United States for $348 ($87 per trip) or eight tickets for $592 ($74 per trip). You must use them up within a year of purchase; they are nontransferable and nonrefundable after you have taken one flight.

With the coupons, you may fly only on Tuesdays, Wednesdays, Thursdays, and Saturdays. And you cannot fly during a three-week blackout period surrounding the Christmas–New Year holidays. You may accumulate frequent-flyer credits for the flights taken with a coupon.

For information: Call 1-800-251-5720.

TWA

This airline offers two choices. One is the TWA Senior Travel Card, which is simple enough: for a one-time fee of $25, a person who is at least 62 receives a discount of 10 percent on the price of any TWA ticket, even the cheapest, to most TWA destinations, including Hawaii, Alaska, the Caribbean, and Europe. For an additional lifetime fee of $75, you get a companion option that allows a travel companion of any age, who may differ on each trip, to get the same discount. With the card, you'll qualify for frequent-flyer points, discounts on car rentals, and a travel newsletter.

The second option is TWA's VSP Senior Pass, which for $1,399 per person allows you, at 65, a year's unlimited travel within the continental United States and Puerto Rico. A pass for a younger companion is available at the same price. Members may also buy international options to fly outside the country. For example, an additional $499 currently gets you a round-trip to most of Europe and the Middle East. And for about $199, you can add a round-trip to the Bahamas.

VSP Pass holders are eligible for discounts on certain brand-name products, hotels, and car rentals but are not eligible for mileage credits.

There are a few restrictions to consider. Among them: You may travel between the same two domestic cities no more than three times during the year. Travel is limited to midweek and Saturdays. Seats are limited. Blackouts at peak holiday periods apply. Pass holders must book flights between 7 and 21 days in advance.
For information: Call your travel agent or 1-800-221-2000.

UNITED AIRLINES

United's senior travel club, called Silver Wings Plus, is designed for those over 60 (although you don't get discounted fares until you are 65). For $50, you can become a member and receive two $25 discount certificates that may be applied to any flight taken within a year. For an additional $150, you may also acquire a lifetime companion membership and two more discount certificates worth $50 each. Your traveling companion (who may be different on each trip) gets the same privileges you do.

With your membership, you'll get discounts on hotels, rental cars, and travel packages. You will be automatically enrolled in the frequent-flyer program, get bonus miles, and receive a quarterly newsletter.

And when you are 65, you (and your traveling companion, if you choose that option) get 10 percent off any fare in the United States, the Bahamas, Canada, Mexico, Singapore, Thailand, Korea, and the Philippines. The same discount applies on United Express, British Airways, and Lufthansa flights to Europe.

For information: Call your travel agent or 1-800-628-2868.

US AIR

This airline's no-fee, no-hassle Senior Saver Program is very simple and straightforward: it gives you and a companion 10 percent off on any and all fares. Just ask for it if you are over 65 and provide a valid ID when you pick up your tickets. You may accumulate mileage credits in the frequent-flyer program when you use the discount.

For information: Call your travel agent or 1-800-428-4322.

U.S. REGIONAL AIRLINES

ALASKA AIRLINES
Alaska Airlines applies a discount schedule to fares in and out of Alaska for travelers 60 and older. The percentage varies according to destination.
For information: Call 1-800-426-0333.

ALOHA
Aloha flies only among the Hawaiian Islands. It gives a discount to people over 65.
For information: Call 1-800-367-5250.

HAWAIIAN AIR
Another interisland airline, Hawaiian Air offers, instead of the current regular adult fare of $44.95, a fare of $39.95 for the same flight to folks over 65.
For information: Call 1-800-367-5320.

MIDWEST EXPRESS
This airline offers the same deal as PSA.
For information: Call 1-800-452-2022.

PSA
A West Coast carrier, PSA gives those over 65 a 10 percent discount on all fares to most of its destinations.
For information: Call 1-800-435-9772.

SUNWORLD
Sunworld, which flies in the West and offers free stopovers in Las Vegas, gives 10 percent off and double frequent-flyer credits to over-60s on any fare, Monday

through Thursday plus Saturday. A traveling companion, any age, gets the same. A second Sunworld option is the Super 60 Funpass, good for unlimited travel for a year, anytime, any day, at a cost of $800.
For information: Call 1-800-722-4111.

WHAT'S DOING IN CANADIAN SKIES

AIR CANADA

Now here's a really good deal. If you're over 60, you get substantial discounts on flights between Canada and Florida; if you're over 65, you get them on all routes in Canada and the United States. The discounts vary with the route and travel time, but generally they amount to 50 percent off the regular tourist fares in the high season (June to September and holiday periods; to Florida, this means the winter months) and up to 60 percent in off-peak seasons. You must buy your tickets at least 14 days before traveling and stay over at least one Sunday. You will be asked for proof of age upon purchase and again at the airport. Remember, before you buy, check this fare against any promotional "seat sales."

Air Canada is currently testing another senior program, a summertime promotion available only to Canadians. Called the Gadabout, it treats people over 65 and traveling companions of any age to unlimited multistop travel to 80 destinations (except Florida) on Air Canada and its partner carriers. Only one stopover is permitted in each city. The Gadabout ticket costs $500.
For information: Call 1-800-422-6232.

CANADIAN AIRLINES INTERNATIONAL

A recent merger of several airlines, Canadian Airlines International gives seniors over 65 a great discount of 50 to 60 percent on just about all fares on domestic flights within Canada. This beats most other super-saver fares, although often a "seat sale" will produce a far lower price. To get the senior discount, you must book two weeks in advance and have proof of age. There are no restrictions on time, day, or season.
For information: Call 1-800-426-7000.

GOOD DEALS ON FOREIGN AIRLINES

Again, always inquire about special senior discounts when you book a flight, because airlines often change their policies without much notice. Your travel agent can provide current information.

FINNAIR

This airline gives great discounts on flights from New York or Los Angeles to Helsinki. For example, as we go to press, you can fly round-trip from New York to Helsinki for $248 one way, $496 round-trip, if you are at least 65. These fares compare to a regular one-way rate of $829 and $720 for an Apex round-trip fare. The catch is that you cannot book your flight until three days before departure. However, the fares are available year-round, and you may take along a companion at the same price.
For information: Call 1-800-223-5700.

KLM ROYAL DUTCH AIRLINES

KLM lowers the fares somewhat for travelers over 60 and their spouses of any age on flights from New York to several cities in the Netherlands—but only in the off-season, usually from October until the end of May. You must buy your tickets less than three days before you fly.

For information: Call your travel agent or 1-800-556-7777.

MEXICANA

Discounts for seniors apply to all Mexicana fares, even the lowest "peso saver" fares, and on all international flights. This means flights from 11 U.S. gateway cities to 34 points in Mexico, Central America, and the Caribbean. A 10 percent reduction is given during the high season (December through April; July and August) and 20 percent the rest of the year. To qualify, you must be 65 (your traveling companion may be any age and will get the same discount) and prove your age when you buy your ticket and board the plane.

For information: Call your travel agent or 1-800-531-7921.

SAS

If you're 65, this airline and its subsidiary, LIN, charge you only $30 for one-way direct flights between cities in Sweden, no matter the distance from Stockholm. If you must change planes in Stockholm or Sundsvall en route from southern Sweden to northern Sweden or vice versa, you pay $60 in each direction.

For information: Call your travel agent or 1-800-221-2350.

TAP AIR PORTUGAL

If you're over 60, you may fly at a discount on advance-purchase tickets on round-trip flights from New York or Boston to Lisbon, Pôrto, or Faro, as well as Madeira and the Azores. Your traveling companion gets the same fare. But there are some restrictions. The discount applies only during the off-season, from September 1 until the end of May, and there are some blackouts around the Christmas holidays. You must buy your tickets 14 days in advance and fly only on Friday, Saturday, or Sunday. Return may be on any day of the week after a minimum stay of seven days.

For information: Call a travel agent or 1-800-221-7370.

Chapter Eight

Beating the Costs of Car Rentals

Never rent a car without getting a discount or a special promotional rate. Almost all car-rental agencies in the United States and Canada give them to all manner of customers, including those who belong to over-50 organizations (see Chapter 20) and airline senior clubs (see Chapter 7). The discount that's coming to you as a member can save you a lot of money. Refer to the membership material sent by the group to which you belong for specific information about your discount privileges.

But, first, keep in mind:

▶ Don't grab your member discount too hastily because you may belong to some other organization that will save you even more. Or specials may be offered that week or month that prove to be even better deals. So, always ask for the *best rate available* at that moment—mentioning, of course, the groups to which you belong.
▶ When you call to ask about rates or reservations, always be armed with your organization's ID number and your own membership card for reference.
▶ The savings may not be available at all locations, so you must check them out each time you make a reservation.

Enough advice. Here are the car-rental agencies that are currently offering you special rates or discounts.

ALAMO
You can get a special rate at Alamo Rent-a-Car if you belong to the September Days Club operated by Days Inns for people over 50.
For information: Call 1-800-327-9633.

AMERICAN INTERNATIONAL
This company's news is that it gives members of AARP a discount of 10 percent on the regular domestic rates and 15 percent on the counter rates at international locations.
For information: Call 1-800-527-0202.

AVIS
Special rates, amounting to 5 to 10 percent off regular rates, are given to members of AARP, CARP (Canadian Association of Retired Persons), and American Airlines' Senior SAAvers Club.
For information: Call 1-800-331-1800.

BUDGET/SEARS RENT-A-CAR
Budget/Sears gives discounts to members of Mature Outlook, American Airlines Senior SAAvers Club, AARP, and many other lesser-known 50-plus or senior groups. The usual saving is $5 per day on weekday rates and $2 per day on weekly and weekend rates.
For information: Call 1-800-527-0700.

DOLLAR
Discounts, which vary according to location, are offered to AARP members at 50 and anyone else over 60.
For information: Call 1-800-421-6868.

GENERAL RENT-A-CAR
Through an arrangement with AARP and Eastern Airline's Get-Up-and-Go Passport, General gives members of both groups 10 percent off the regular rates.
For information: Call 1-800-327-7607.

HERTZ

If you are a member of AARP, Mature Outlook, or Y.E.S., you will be entitled to savings, usually from 5 to 10 percent, on Hertz rental cars. In addition, Hertz gives discounts to members of United Airlines' Silver Wings Plus club, TWA's Senior Travel Card, Piedmont Airlines' Senior Class Travel Club, Days Inns' September Days Club, and Holiday Inns' Travel Venture Club. **For information:** Call 1-800-654-3131.

NATIONAL

With this rent-a-car agency, you can get special rates and discounts if you are a member of Mature Outlook, AARP, American Airlines' Senior SAAvers, Days Inns' September Days Club, and Holiday Inns' Travel Venture Club. Also, Continental Airline's Golden Travelers Club members receive a 10 percent reduction on regular rates. **For information:** Call 1-800-328-5800.

THRIFTY RENT-A-CAR

AARP members traveling in the United States get special rates (with 150 free miles per day) and 5 percent off the regular rates overseas. CARP and Days Inns' September Days Club members receive the same rates, while those who belong to Continental Airline's Golden Travelers Club are entitled to 10 percent off the rates as well as a certificate redeemable for a four-day weekend rental with 250 free miles from $65 for subcompacts to $115 for luxury cars. **For information:** Call 1-800-FOR-CARS.

Chapter Nine

Saving a Bundle on Trains and Buses in North America

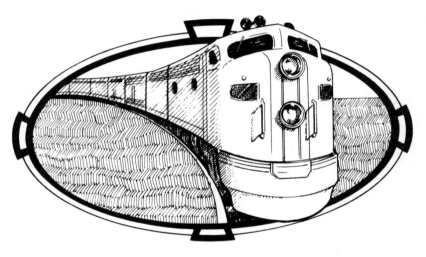

Getting around town, especially if you live in a city where driving is not a practical option, probably means depending on public transportation to get you from hither to yon. Remember that, once you reach a particular birthday—in most cases, your 60th or 65th—you can take advantage of some good senior markdowns on trains, buses, and subways (unfortunately taxis have yet to join the movement). All you need is a senior ID card issued by your city or county to play this game which usually reduces fares by half. Although you may find it uncomfortable at the beginning to pull out that card and flash it at the bus driver or ticket agent, it soon becomes automatic and you will realize some nice savings.

Seniors can find bargains on long-distance rail and bus travel as well.

RIDING THE RAILS

Probably every commuter railroad in the United States and Canada gives older riders a break, although you may have to do your traveling during off-peak periods when the trains are not filled with go-getters rushing to and from their offices. Ask for your discount when you purchase your ticket.

As for serious long-distance travel, many mature travelers are addicted to the railroads, finding riding the rails a leisurely, relaxed, romantic, comfortable, economical, and satisfying way to make miles while enjoying the scenery.

So many passes and discounts on railroads are available to travelers heading for other parts of the world that sorting them out becomes confusing. But, once you do, they will help stretch your dollars while covering a lot of ground.

See the country-by-country section in Chapter 4 for the best deals on trains in foreign countries for travelers of a certain age.

AMTRAK

To lure mature travelers, Amtrak now offers a discount of 25 percent on regular one-way fares to people over 65. You must buy your ticket before boarding the train and be ready to prove your age. Remember that there are blackout periods when this fare isn't available; these are usually during the major holidays or other peak travel seasons.

Now, some words of wisdom: Do not assume that the senior fare is the best bargain. Always mention the senior discount, but be sure you get the *lowest fare available*. On Amtrak's family fare, for example, one member of a couple traveling together pays full fare, the other half fare. (Children 12 through 21 pay half fare, and children 2 through 11 pay only 25 percent.) Thus the cost to a couple is the same (25 percent off), but the blackout periods do not apply; you may travel at these family fare rates year-round, any day, any time.

Other good deals include the All Aboard America fares. Here the United States is divided into three regions—eastern, central, and western. As we go to press, you can travel round-trip anywhere within one region for $138 to $159, in two contiguous regions for $188 to

$239, and in the entire system for $238 to $299, depending on the time of year.

In other words, do your homework before buying your tickets.

For information: Call Amtrak at 1-800-USA-RAIL.

VIA RAIL CANADA

The government-owned Canadian passenger railroad offers those 60 and over a one-third reduction on the regular coach fare, one way or round-trip, every day of the year, with no restrictions—not even on Christmas Day. The discount does not apply to club seats or sleepers.

In the off-season, however, a better deal is Via Rail's Apex Continental Saver, which anyone can get, whatever his or her age. This gives a 40 percent discount on both the basic fare and club chairs or sleepers. The catch is that this special fare is not available in the peak summer season, usually June through September. And tickets must be purchased a week in advance.

Another possible cheaper fare is the one-day round-trip excursion fare between major Canadian cities. The catch? The trip must be made in one calendar day and may not occur on a Friday.

For information: Call Via Rail Canada's toll-free numbers, which differ for each region of the country. Get the number for your area by dialing 1-800-555-1212.

LET THEM DO THE DRIVING: GOING BY BUS

Never, never board a bus without showing the driver your senior ID card, because even the smallest bus lines in the tiniest communities in this country and abroad give senior discounts, usually half fare. In Europe, your senior rail pass is often valid on major motorcoach lines as well, so always be sure to ask.

As for the big boys on this continent . . .

GREYHOUND LINES

This national bus line is currently making a test run of its brand-new Greyhound Golden Savers Seniors Club, offering membership to West Coast (California, Utah, Arizona, Washington, Oregon, Nevada, and Idaho) residents who have reached their 55th birthdays. If the club pans out there, membership will open up to everyone in the country.

Here's how it works: After getting a membership card by filling out an application available at any Greyhound location or via newspaper coupons (there may be a small one-time handling charge) and providing proof of age, club members are entitled to a 15 percent discount on any fare anywhere Greyhound goes in the United States. They will also receive a quarterly newsletter that outlines additional offerings such as tour packages, hotel discounts, and special promotional fares.

Those who are not lucky enough to live in those Western states will, in the meantime, receive a 10 percent discount on any fare, any day of the year in the United States and Canada, if they are 65 and show proof of age when purchasing their tickets.

For information: Call your local Greyhound office.

TRAILWAYS

We're listing this bus line separately, even though it is in the process of merging with Greyhound, because some bus routes retain the name. The senior perk of a 10 percent discount for those over 65 applies even when the motorcoach is labeled Trailways. And, if the Golden Savers Seniors Club passes the test and becomes a nationwide reality, its benefits will be extended to Trailways passengers too.

GRAY LINE TOURS

This is an association of many small independent motorcoach lines throughout the country, all of which offer sight-seeing and package tours. Most, but not all, of them give a 15 percent discount on half- and full-day sight-seeing tours to members of AARP (in which case you need be only 50 years old—see Chapter 20) and sometimes other groups as well. Find out if you qualify before buying your ticket.

For information: Call the Gray Line Tours office in your area.

VOYAGEUR

This Canadian motorcoach line's Club 60 offers you one-third off regular fares on its regular bus service throughout the provinces of Ontario and Quebec. No need to join anything; simply present proof that you are 60 when you buy your tickets. No restrictions on day or time. You'll also get a discount on Voyageur's one-day tours by bus or riverboat out of such major cities as Montreal, Ottawa, and Toronto.

A really good deal, one that may profit you even more than your one-third discount if you plan to do considerable wandering in these provinces, is the TourPass. For $9 a day for 15 consecutive days between May 1 and October 15 (a total of $135), you get unlimited travel on all of Voyageur's lines as well as those of 47 other carriers in both provinces.

For information: Call the Voyageur office in your area.

ONTARIO NORTHLAND

This is an excursion railroad that takes you on wilderness tours of Canada's north country through areas accessible only by rail or plane—and it offers mature travelers some fine price reductions. For example, the Polar Bear Express, an excursion from Cochrane, Ontario, to Moosonee near James Bay, operates from the end of June until Labor Day except on Fridays and sells senior tickets for 50 percent off the regular fare.

For information: Ontario Northland, 65 Front Street West, Toronto, Ontario M5J 1E6; 1-800-268-9281 or 415-965-4268.

Chapter Ten

Hotels and Motels: Get Your Over-50 Markdowns

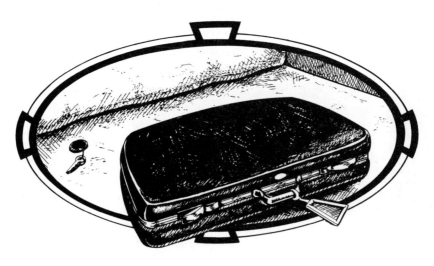

Across the United States and Canada, major chains of hotels and motels (and individual establishments as well) are chasing the mature market. (That's you.) As a candidate for an increasing barrage of bargains in lodgings, you may not have to sell all the family jewels to afford your next trip.

To get your discounts at most establishments, all that's required is evidence that you are 55, or 60, or 65, as the case may be. Or that you are a member of a club that makes many of the same savings available to you at 50. When you join the American Association of Retired Persons, (you needn't be retired), Mature Outlook, or a similar organization, you will receive a list of the lodging chains that offer special rates. See Chapter 20 for information about these organizations.

But, first, keep in mind:

If you want to take advantage of the discounts coming to you, be sure to do some advance scouting and planning with your travel agent or on your own.

▶ In this rapidly changing world, rates and policies can be altered in a flash, so an update is always advisable.
▶ Information about discounts is seldom volunteered; in most cases, you must arrange for them when you make your reservations and remind the desk clerk of them again when you check in. Do not wait until you're settling your bill because then it may be too late.
▶ It's quite possible that a special promotional rate, especially in off-peak seasons or on weekends, may save you more money than your senior discount. Many hotels, especially in big cities and warm climes, cut

their prices drastically in the summer, for example. Others that cater mostly to business people during the week try to encourage weekend traffic by offering bargain rates if you stay over a Saturday night. So always investigate all the possibilities before you get too enthusiastic about using your hard-earned discount, and remember to ask for the *lowest available rate.*

▶ There are several chains of no-frills budget motels that don't offer discounts or too much in the way of amenities but do charge very low room rates and tend to be located along the most-traveled routes.

▶ In most cases, not every hotel or inn in a chain will offer the discount. Those that do are called "participating" hotels/motels.

▶ In addition to the chains, many individual hotels and inns are eager for your business and offer special reduced rates. Always *ask* before making a reservation. Your travel agent should be able to help you with this.

▶ By the way, your discount will not be given on top of other special discounts. One discount is all you get.

BEST WESTERN

This huge chain of independently owned motels gives a 10 percent discount on your rates at most of its properties if you are over 55. Advance reservations are required, and so is proof of age when you check in.
For information: Call 1-800-528-1234.

DAYS INNS

One of the largest lodging chains in the country, Days Inns invites people over 50 to join its September Days Club, which entitles you to 15 to 50 percent off rooms at

about 250 participating hotels, motels, and lodges. You also get 10 percent off your meals at Days Inns restaurants and your purchases at its gift shops; discounts on rental cars from Hertz, Alamo, National, and Thrifty; discounted prescription drugs; trips and escorted tours at group rates; information on last-minute travel bargains; a quarterly magazine; and a lot more perks. Membership costs $12 a year per person or couple.
For information: Call 1-800-241-5050.

DOUBLETREE HOTELS

These luxury hotels are concentrated in the west and give senior discounts to AARP members and others, but each determines its own policy, so you'll have to check the specific hotel that interests you to find out what it offers.
For information: Call 1-800-528-0444.

DRURY INNS

These budget motels offer a 10 percent discount on the regular room rates at all of their locations to those who are 55-plus. Just ask and have proof of age handy.
For information: Call 1-800-325-8300.

ECONO LODGES

With a string of about 400 budget motels on the East Coast, this chain provides a 10 percent discount at most of its properties to anybody over 55. It also has a Frequent Travelers Plan: for every six nights you spend within one year at the same participating motel, you get seven free nights.
For information: Call 1-800-446-6900.

ECONOMY INNS OF AMERICA

An economy lodging chain, with motels located near major highways in California, Florida, and Georgia, it gives 10 percent off the already cheap room rates to people over 55. Just ask for it.

For information: Call 1-800-826-0778.

EMBASSY SUITES HOTELS

These feature two-room suites with free breakfast and complimentary cocktails and take 10 percent off the regular room rates for members of AARP, the National Retired Teachers Association, the National Council of Senior Citizens, and holders of Silver Savers Passports—that is, if they are participating in the program. If you're not a card holder, you'll get the discount anyway if you're over 65.

For information: Call 1-800-362-2779.

HAMPTON INNS

The LifeStyle 50 program which offers a four-for-one deal for people over 50 has only recently been initiated by this chain of hotels. Membership in LifeStyle 50 means a guest may share a room (two double beds) with three other adults over 50 at any of the 145 Hampton Inns around the country and pay only the *single* rate. Now there's a novel idea! Simply flash your AARP, NRTA, NARFE, or other ID card when you check in or apply for a LifeStyle 50 membership card by phone.

For information: Call 1-800-HAMPTON.

HILTON HOTELS

Hilton has just begun its brand-new Hilton Senior Traveler Program, offering a really good deal to those of us over 60. Once you join, you will get up to 50 percent off the room rates at all of the participating hotels in this chain of almost 300 properties. There are additional perks to your membership, too, such as a newspaper at your door every morning and late checkout privileges.

For information: Call 1-800-445-8667.

HOLIDAY INNS

There are a few ways you can cut down on your hotel bill here. You can join the Holiday Inn Travel Venture Club for $10 a year if you are 55-plus and get 20 percent off your room rates at nearly 1,000 participating hotels. Membership also entitles you to 10 percent off your meals at Holiday Inn restaurants, discounts on Hertz and National rental cars, and a 5 to 10 percent discount on Northwest Airlines flights. You can get an application for the club at a Holiday Inn or by phone.

The same 20 percent discount on room rates and 10 percent discount on restaurant charges are available to members of Mature Outlook. AARP members get a 10 percent discount on room rates, and some hotels give discounts to Silver Pages Passport holders (see Chapter 16 for information about getting the Passport).

For information: Call 1-800-HOLIDAY for an application for the Holiday Inn Travel Venture Club.

HOWARD JOHNSON

Older travelers are a very important segment of this chain's clientele, and so it has launched a special program featuring TV weatherman Willard Scott as spokesperson. Called Howard Johnson Road Rally, it offers up to 50 percent off regular room rates to people over 60 or to card-carrying members of national seniors organizations like AARP and Mature Outlook, in which case the offer goes to people over 50. Just check into a participating HJ and show your ID.

For each night, you'll get a checkpoint; collect three of these, send the evidence to Road Rally, and you get a booklet filled with money-saving coupons for both travel and merchandise, plus an entry into a sweepstakes contest for a new car, a dinner with Willard Scott, or a weekend vacation.

Book ahead to get the top half-price rooms because, at some times of the year, the number of such rooms is limited. But, in any case, you will always get at least 15 percent off.
For information: Call 1-800-634-3464.

HYATT HOTELS
These are all individually owned; therefore, each one offers its own discounts. Those in big cities or major resort areas rarely have senior rates, but others may take 25 to 50 percent off the room rate for up to four people in a room. Hotels in resort areas tend to make their most generous offers in the off-season.
For information: Call 1-800-228-9000.

IMPERIAL 400 INNS
A chain of budget motels, Imperial 400 Inns takes 10 percent off the room rates for members of AARP or other "senior citizens."
For information: Call 1-800-368-4400.

INN SUITES

With locations in Arizona and California, this chain has a Silver Passport Program for travelers over 55. You may enroll at any of the inns and receive a membership card good for future stays. What it gets you is 10 percent off regular room rates on the one- and two-room suites Monday through Thursday and 15 percent off on Friday, Sunday, and holidays, plus complimentary breakfast and a morning newspaper. The *Silver Passport News*, a quarterly, keeps you up to date.
For information: Call 1-800-842-4242.

KNIGHTS INNS/ARBORGATE INNS

This budget motel chain with about 110 locations in the Southeast, gives a discount of 10 percent to anyone over 55 throughout the year.
For information: Call 614-866-1569.

LA QUINTA MOTOR INNS

These nearly 200 locations mostly in the Sunbelt are inexpensive, and they become even more so when you ask for your 15 percent discount. You'll get it if you are a member of AARP, Mature Outlook, or a similar organization—or if you are 55 and can prove it. It is sometimes not available during special events in a particular location.
For information: Call 1-800-531-5900.

LK MOTELS

A budget chain in middle America, it takes 10 percent off for AARP members and anybody else who's over 55.
For information: Call 1-800-848-5767.

RESTAURANT DISCOUNTS

Many restaurants offer discounts to people in their prime, but in most cases you'll have to seek them out yourself, by asking, watching the ads in your local newspaper, or looking in *The Silver Pages* for your area (see Chapter 16). But here are four large chains that offer them to you at age 50:

Denny's has a Seniors' Menu with 22 breakfast, lunch, and dinner dishes to choose from and a dinner special that changes every day. The portions are reduced and so are the prices, because research has found that many eaters over 50 are watching their weight or don't have ravenous appetites.

Holiday Inn restaurants give a discount of 10 percent on your food bill if you belong to Mature Outlook (see Chapter 20) or the Holiday Inn Travel Venture Club (see Chapter 19).

Ponderosa restaurants, all 600 of them, will take 10 percent off any regular menu items (in other words, food that isn't a "special")—from a cup of coffee to a complete meal—if you show your Mature Outlook card when you pay your bill.

The restaurants in **Red Lion Inns** and **Thunderbird Motor Inns** will reduce your food bill by 15 percent on regular-priced items if you have a membership card for AARP or Mature Outlook or a Silver Savers' Passport.

MARRIOTT

Marriott's Leisurelife Program may be one of the best deals around. It gives you, at age 62, rooms at 50 percent off regular weekday rates for single, double, or family accommodations seven days a week. You may reserve up to two rooms at half price so family members or friends traveling with you can share your good fortune. There's also a 25 percent discount on dining (except on specials and alcoholic beverages) for your entire party of up to eight people. The dining discount may be used as often as you like, as may a 10 percent discount on gift-shop purchases at any of Marriott's hotels and resorts. There are no membership fees or cards. You simply request the discount and present proof of age. What's more, you need not be a hotel guest to get the restaurant discount.

Advance room reservations are required. One hitch: the room discounts may not be available at all times, especially in peak seasons when there is high demand. **For information:** Call 1-800-228-9290.

NENDELS MOTOR INNS

A Pacific Northwest chain that takes 10 percent off the regular room rates for members of all senior organizations. Request the discount when you make your reservation or check in.
For information: Call 1-800-547-0106.

OMNI HOTELS

Formerly Dunfey Hotels, this chain is another winner. Its participating hotels—23 of them—offer AARP members a 50 percent discount on regular room rates any night of the week, based on space availability, with complimentary continental breakfast for both you and your traveling companion sharing the room. You'll also get 15 percent off food and nonalcoholic beverages in the hotel restaurants. To receive the discount, reserve ahead, request the special discount, and be ready to

provide your AARP card number. At check-in, you will be asked to show your membership card. In the restaurants, present your card before you order.
For information: Call 1-800-THE-OMNI.

QUALITY INNS/COMFORT INNS/ CLARION HOTELS AND RESORTS

All part of Quality Inns International's worldwide operation of more than 900 hotels, they offer their Prime Time program, good for 10 percent off the room rates any day of the year, to guests who are members of AARP, Mature Outlook, or NARCUP, or who are over 60. The discount applies to the company's all-suite hotels as well as hotels and motels. A booklet, *Tips for Travelers over 55*, is also distributed to guests who request it.
For information: Call 1-800-221-2222.

RADISSON HOTELS

Radisson will give you and your roommates 25 percent off regular rates at all of its 90 locations in the United States and Mexico if you belong to Mature Outlook, AARP, or the Silver & Gold Program, or are 65. Mention the discount when you reserve the room and again when you check in.
For information: Call 1-800-228-9822.

RAMADA

Ramada's Best Years Program is a good deal for you if you belong to any of a long list of "senior" organizations, including the over-50 clubs, or are over 60. It entitles you to 25 percent off the room rates in almost

500 participating Ramada motor inns and hotels. There may be blackout periods, so reserve ahead.
For information: Call 1-800-272-6232.

RED CARPET INNS/MASTER HOSTS INNS/ SCOTTISH INNS

All operated by Hospitality International, those in the United States and Canada participate in giving AARP members and anybody else who's 55 a 10 percent discount on room rates year-round, except perhaps during special local events such as spring break in Daytona Beach.
For information: Call 1-800-251-1962.

RED LION INNS/THUNDERBIRD MOTOR INNS

To over-50s who present AARP, Mature Outlook, or Silver Pages Passport cards, Red Lions and Thunderbirds—all in the western states—give their Prime Rate, which amounts to 20 percent off the regular room rates. Book ahead because there are occasional blackout periods. In addition, their restaurants give you 15 percent off food chosen from the regular menu, except on holidays.
For information: Call 1-800-547-8010.

RELAX INNS

Sprinkled around Canada, these hotels give guests over 55 a nice break. Here you are charged the single corporate rate for a room, no matter how many people (up to four) occupy it. At one of the hotels, for example, a four-person room would normally cost $64, but you would get it for $50.
For information: Call 1-800-661-9563.

RODEWAY INNS
With about 150 locations in the United States, Canada, and Mexico, Rodeway Inns ask only that you be 55 in order to get their 10 percent discount. Request the discount when you make your reservation.
For information: Call 1-800-533-2100.

SANDMAN HOTELS AND INNS
All situated in western Canada, these take 25 percent off the regular room rate if you are 55 or over.
For information: Call 1-800-663-6900.

SHERATON HOTELS
With more than 500 establishments in 62 countries, Sheraton gives AARP members at 50, or anybody else at 55, a good break: a 25 percent discount at all of its participating hotels worldwide. You'll need advance reservations and proper identification. Although the discount may be offered at any time of year, it may not be available at peak periods.
For information: Call 1-800-325-3535.

SHONEY'S INNS
Shoney's Inns are inexpensive motels concentrated in the South. Because each inn is a franchise operation, policies vary, but most take 10 percent off for members of AARP or Mature Outlook and others with a driver's license that shows them to be over 50.
For information: Call 1-800-222-2222.

SONESTA INTERNATIONAL HOTELS
This collection of 11 luxury hotels gives members of AARP a 10 percent discount at two of its establish-

ments and a 15 percent discount at six others, including the one in Amsterdam. Request yours when you make your reservations.

For information: Call 1-800-343-7170.

STOUFFER HOTELS
Stouffer has a Great Years program that gives guests over 60 a room for $59 (or sometimes less) per night, single or double occupancy, any day of the week, year-round. In many cases, this amounts to about half the regular rate. However, rooms are limited to availability, and the special rate does not apply to the five Stouffer resorts. Advance reservations are required.

For information: Call 1-800-HOTELS-1.

TRAVELODGE/VISCOUNT
Fifteen percent off the room rates is what's offered by this large group of motor inns and hotels if you are a member of just about any 50-plus organization, both the usual and unusual ones, or American Airlines Silver SAAvers Club. The discount is good anytime, so mention your membership when you make reservations and/or check in.

For information: Call 1-800-255-3050.

TREADWAY INNS
A small group of hotels in the East, Treadway Inns have discounts for senior citizens or members of such organizations as AARP and Mature Outlook. The savings vary from hotel to hotel but amount to about 10 to 15 percent. Ask for yours when you make reservations.

For information: Call 1-800-631-0182.

VAGABOND INNS

Concentrated on the West Coast, this chain has its Club 55 for mature travelers over 55 that offers a special rate of about 10 to 15 percent off the regular room rate. For a $10 registration fee, you get a bag of gifts plus $10 in coupons good toward a stay at any Vagabond Inn. Members are invited to a series of monthly events at special rates at various Vagabond Inns in California and Nevada. There have been, for example, a Mexican Fiesta party weekend and a Basque Bash and Golf Tournament. The club is also organizing tour packages, such as the 16-day Western Adventure that takes members to the Canadian Rockies. A newsletter keeps you up-to-date.

For information: The Vagabond Inns Club 55, Box 85011, San Diego, CA 92138; 1-800-522-1555.

WESTIN HOTELS & RESORTS

These luxury hotels often offer senior rates (up to 50 percent off regular prices), but each has its own policy, so always ask about it when you make your reservations. If there is no senior discount, ask for the corporate rate, which is 20 to 25 percent off. If you belong to United Airlines Silver Wings Plus, no problem. You'll get a 50 percent reduction.

For information: Call 1-800-228-3000.

WESTMARK HOTELS

Formerly Sheffield Hotels, these hotels are located in Alaska and the Yukon. If you're at least 65, they will give you rooms for $49 to $59 a night, much less than the usual rate, but only in the off-season when it's really chilly up there—October 1 through April 30.

For information: Call 1-800-544-0970.

Chapter Eleven
Alternative Lodgings for Thrifty Wanderers

If you're willing to be innovative, imaginative, and occasionally fairly spartan, you can travel for a song or thereabouts. Here are some novel lodgings that can save you money and, at the same time, supply you with adventures worth talking about for years. They are not all designed specifically for people over 50, but each reports that a good portion of its clientele consists of free spirits of a certain age who are looking to beat the high cost of travel, meet people from other places, and have a real good time.

For more ways to cut travel costs and get smart in the bargain, check out the residential/educational programs in Chapter 15.

THE EVERGREEN CLUB

This is a bed-and-breakfast club for singles or couples over 50 who have guest rooms in their homes that they're willing to make available to fellow club members traveling through their areas. No matter how elegant or simple your home is, no matter how close or far from the beaten path, the visitors pay $10 per night for single accommodations and $15 for double. You may not get rich on this scheme, but you will meet a lot of interesting people. And, in return, you may stay in other people's homes at the same prices when you're on the road.

Organized just a few years ago, the Evergreen Club now includes inexpensive, comfortable accommodations in about 400 homes in nearly every state, as well as Canada, Mexico, and a few European countries.

The first year's dues of $25 ($35 for overseas members) provide a membership card, a directory, and quarterly newsletters. The directory gives names and addresses of members, occupations and interests, policies about pets and smoking, and listings of nearby special attractions. Members make their own reservations and arrangements.

For information: Send a self-addressed, stamped envelope to the Evergreen Club, PO Box 44094, Washington, DC 20026; 703-237-9777.

INNter LODGING CO-OP

Yet another way of sharing your home with other travelers and parlaying that guest room into virtually free lodging for yourself when you travel in the United States, Canada, and Europe. Guests pay $4 or $5 per adult per night, depending upon whether there are private bathroom facilities. Children, who must arrive with their own sleeping bags, are an extra 25¢ a night. You must make your own arrangements directly with the hosts or the travelers who wish to stay with you.

When you join ($45), you receive a membership card and a directory of participating hosts. Anyone any age may join, but the plan tends to appeal most to young families and mature travelers.

For information: INNter Lodging Co-op Services, PO Box 7044, Tacoma, WA 98407-0044; 206-756-0343.

SENIOR VACATION HOTELS OF FLORIDA

These hotels take a novel approach, with one-month minimum vacation packages at a choice of four different hotels for seniors only (in Bradenton, Lakeland, and St. Petersburg). These are all-inclusive, with all meals, transportation, excursions, boat trips, entertainment, parties, and activities in the bundle. Current rates are $700 (single) and $900 (per person, double) for a month in November, December, and April; a little more in January, February, or March. While the hotels will certainly accept you at age 50, you'll fit into the group more snugly if you're a bit more than that.

For information: Senior Vacation Hotels of Florida, 7401 Central Ave., St. Petersburg, FL 33710; 1-800-247-2203 (in Canada, 1-800-843-3713).

SERVAS

Servas is "an international cooperative system of hosts and travelers established to help build world peace, goodwill, and understanding . . . among people of diverse cultures and backgrounds." A nonprofit, nongovernmental, interracial, and interfaith organization open to all ages, it provides lists of hosts, along with their activities and interests, all over the United States as well as the rest of the world. You make your own arrangements to stay with them, usually for two days, and share their everyday lives and concerns. No money changes hands. The hospitable people who take you in do this so they may enjoy your company and learn about you and your culture. You do the same for other travelers in return. For travelers, there is a tax-deductible contribution of $30 to cover expenses, and you will be asked for two letters of reference and an interview.

For information: Send a #10 self-addressed, stamped envelope to US Servas, 11 John St., New York, NY 10038; 212-267-0252.

SUN CITY CENTER
Midway between Tampa and Sarasota in Florida, Sun
City Center wants you to find out what a large self-
contained retirement town is all about and offers special vacation packages to give you a sample of life
there. Prices depend on the season, but you may choose
package #1—four days, three nights, daily continental
breakfast, a dinner for two, a round of golf, unlimited
tennis, swimming, club facilities, for $175 to $260 per
couple—or package #2, for seven days, six nights, with
two rounds of golf and the above, at $275 to $475 per
couple. There is no age minimum.
For information: Sunmark Communities, PO Box
5698, Sun City Center, FL 33570; 1-800-237-8200 (in
Florida, 1-800-282-8040).

SUN CITY WEST AND SUN CITY VISTOSO
Located in Arizona, both cousins of the famous Sun
City and run by Del Webb Development Company, they
offer similar deals—inexpensive vacation stays designed to give you a taste of what goes on in these retirement communities, and, of course, to persuade you
to stay.
Sun City West, with about 16,000 inhabitants, is located 14 miles outside of Phoenix. Its Vacation Special
Program gives you a week in a furnished garden apartment and full use of the recreational facilities of the
community that include golf, bowling, swimming, tennis, and a continental breakfast tour of this place and
the already well-known Sun City. For this you pay for
two people: $199 plus tax per week from January 1

through April 30; $399 plus tax from May 1 through September 30; and $299 plus tax from October 1 through December 31. One of you must be over 50.

Sun City Vistoso is 11 miles outside of Tucson, a smaller version planned for 5,000 people, with an 18-hole desert golf course. Again, you are offered a visit at the same rates. Here, one guest must be over 45 and neither of you may be under 19.

For information: Call 1-800-528-2604 (in Arizona, 602-975-2270).

UNIVERSITY BRITAIN

For only $25 a day, this organization offers travelers of all ages dinner, bed, and breakfast in Great Britain during the summer months (July, August, September) and holiday periods (Easter and Christmas). You'll stay on the campuses of universities for as many nights each as you wish, usually in a single room with a wash basin, but sometimes a double room is available. Your choices: Aberystwyth or Cardiff, both in Wales; Dundee, Scotland; Exeter, Keele, Manchester, Norwich, or Durham, all in England. If you go in a group of 25 or more people, you get a guide as well.

An alternative, also open to all ages, is CampusHotels in Scotland, which gives you a choice of eight city and country campus locations averaging about $23 a night, including a full Scottish breakfast.

This company also offers its two-week for-all-ages escorted University Tour of Great Britain, also inexpensive, which includes everything but lunches and puts you up in university dormitories.

For information: Campus Holidays USA, 242 Bellevue Ave., Upper Montclair, NJ 07043; 1-800-526-2915.

UNTOURS

A company named Idyll provides a way to enjoy Europe without cashing in all your CDs. Untour means settling down for a week or two or three in your own apartment situated in an Austrian or Swiss village, a small town in Germany, a flat in London, or a cottage in Scotland or Wales—a home base from which you do your own sight-seeing. Airfare is part of the package. This deal is open to all ages but attracts mostly seniors. All in all, a bargain.

For information: Hal Taussig, Idyll, PO Box 405, Media, PA 19063; 215-565-5242.

Chapter Twelve
Perks in Parks and Other Good News

Here and there throughout the United States and Canada, clever states, provinces and cities have thought up some enticing ideas designed to capture the imagination of people on the other side of 50. Often they are expressing their appreciation of our many contributions to society and simply want to do something nice for us. And sometimes they are trying to lure a few of our vacation dollars to their vicinity, having discovered that we're always out for a good time and know a nice deal when we see one.

But, first, keep in mind:

▶ Before you set forth to visit a new state, it's a good idea to write ahead for free maps, calendars of events, booklets describing sites and scenes of interest, accommodation guides, and perhaps even a list of special discounts or other good things that are available to you as a person in your prime.
▶ Many states offer passes to their state parks and recreation facilities free or at reduced prices to people who are old enough to treat them properly.

After the section on national parks, state park passes and other notable deals are described under each state on the following pages. There may be other good deals that have escaped our attention, but those in this chapter are probably the cream of the crop.

NATIONAL PARKS

GOLDEN AGE PASSPORT

Available to anyone over 62, this is a free lifetime entrance permit to all of the federal government's parks, monuments, and recreation areas that charge entrance fees. Anybody who accompanies you in the same non-commercial vehicle also gets in free. If you turn up at the gate in a commercial vehicle such as a bus, the passport admits you and your spouse, your children, and your parents too, so remember to take them along.

You will also get a 50 percent discount on federal use fees charged for facilities and services such as camping, boat launching, parking, cave tours, etc.

The passport is not available by mail. You must pick one up in person at any National Park System area where entrance fees are charged or at any National Park Service and Forest Service headquarters or regional office, most ranger station offices, Fish and Wildlife Service offices, or National Wildlife Refuges. You must have proof of age. A driver's license will do just fine.

(The Golden Access Passport provides the same benefits for the disabled of any age. The Golden Eagle Passport, for those under 62, costs $25 per year.)

For information: National Park Service, PO Box 37127, Washington, DC 20013.

CANADIAN NATIONAL PARKS

All you have to do to get free entry for day visits is to show your driver's license and vehicle registration. The same is generally true for provincial parks, with half-price camping fees charged on the weekends.

STATE OFFERINGS

For a free listing of all the state tourism offices and their toll-free numbers, send a self-addressed, stamped envelope to Discover America, Travel Industry Association of America, 2 Lafayette Center, 1133 21st St. NW, Washington, DC 20036.

CALIFORNIA

Palm Springs' Super Seniors is a package of programs and activities designed specifically for people over 50. You'll need a valid P.S. Pass (a free pass that gives you a few discounts in Palm Springs and Palm Desert; get yours at the Palm Springs Leisure Center) and $2 a year to join. With a Super Senior stamp on your P.S. Pass card, you'll be in line for a free T-shirt, free admission to a film festival, and discounts on dance lessons, riding lessons, theater admission, ice skating, fitness classes, hikes, dances, and yoga.

For information: Greater Palm Springs Convention and Visitors Bureau, 255 N. El Cielo Rd., Palm Springs, CA 92262-6993; 619-323-8272.

COLORADO

The Aspen Leaf Pass entitles Colorado citizens 62 and over to free entrance to state facilities and free camping on weekdays.

For information: Colorado Tourism Board, 1625 Broadway, Denver, CO 80202; 303-592-5410.

FLORIDA

Orlando/Orange County has its own version of coupon books to entice visitors to the area in the fall. Once offered only to older tourists, now it is available to anyone. The coupons are good for savings on assorted purchases from hotels and motels to lobster dinners.

For information: For a free copy of the *Fall Celebration Coupon Book*, write to Orlando/Orange County Convention and Visitors Bureau, 7680 Republic Dr., Orlando, FL 32819; 305-345-8882.

INDIANA

The Golden Age Pass for those over 60 admits the bearer and all fellow passengers in a private vehicle to all Department of Natural Resources properties. The pass costs $5 a year.

United Senior Action is a statewide political action organization whose primary purpose is to promote legislation and other measures that help older people. In addition to its lobbying function, it has developed a package of benefits for its members, including a prescription drug program, legal services (free consultations with a lawyer plus answers to legal questions), a consumer handbook, and some discounts.

For information: United Senior Action Foundation, 6940 E. 38th St., Indianapolis, IN 46226.

MASSACHUSETTS

The Massachusetts Cultural Coupon Book is not for peppy seniors alone, but it's worth a mention here because it's a good deal. The free coupons offer discounts at about 35 attractions statewide, from the Boston Symphony Orchestra to Tanglewood concerts to the New Bedford Whaling Museum and the JFK Library and Museum in Boston.

The tourism division also publishes a discount lodging packages guide and a two-for-one discount ski brochure.

For information: Massachusetts Division of Tourism, 100 Cambridge St., Boston, MA 02202; 617-727-3201.

GOOD NEWS FOR RVers

Safari Campgrounds and **Yogi Bear Jellystone Camp Resorts** will give you, if you're 60, a 15 percent discount on daily site rental fees at their participating campgrounds sprinkled around the United States and Canada. To get it, you must have an SC identification card. Buy a card when you next stop at a campground or send for it.

For information: Send $2 and proof of age (make a photocopy of your driver's license) to Leisure Systems, 14 S. Third Ave., Sturgeon Bay, WI 54235; 1-800-358-9165.

Cruise America, which rents motor homes and vans, deducts 10 percent from your bill if you flash your AARP card, proving that you are 50 or more. Advance reservations are necessary.

For information: Call 1-800-327-7778 (in Canada and Alaska, 1-800-327-7799).

Some **KOA Kampgrounds** will give you a discount simply because you've joined a 50-plus organization, but most don't—which is OK, because all you need is the KOA Value Card, and that's available to everyone. It will get you 10 percent off the regular registration fees at participating locations. It costs $4 and is available at Kampgrounds or by mail.

For information: Send $4 to KOA Value Card, PO Box 31734 VCD, Billings, MT 59107-1734.

NEW YORK

New York State's Golden Park Pass, good Mondays through Fridays, gives free vehicle access to state parks and recreational facilities to residents who are 62. In addition, it entitles its bearer to free admission to state historic sites and arboretums and a 50 percent reduction on some park activity fees such as swimming and golf.

To go along with the park pass, send for New York's innovative free discount coupon book, *I Love New York Great Vacation Savers*. This saves you money on hotels,

---

The Good Sam Club is an international organization of RVers, mentioned here because the vast majority of people in rolling homes are over 50. This club can be very handy and reassuring when you're cruising the country. Among its benefits are 10 percent discounts on fees at thousands of campgrounds and on propane gas, RV parts and accessories; in addition, it offers a lost-key service, lost-pet service, trip routing, mail-forwarding service, telephone-message service, a magazine, caravan gatherings, and campground directories. Probably the most important benefit is the emergency road service available to members because it includes towing for any vehicle, no matter how large. That's hard to get. Also, there are Good Sam travel tours all over the world, many of them "caraventures." And not least, about 2,000 local chapters hold regular outings, meetings, and campouts. Membership costs $15 a year per family.

For information: The Good Sam Club, PO Box 500, Agoura, CA 91301; 1-800-423-5061 (in California, 1-800-382-3455).

motels, attractions, museums, car rentals, camp-grounds, and more.
For information: For a free coupon book, contact Savers, Box 992, Latham, NY 12110; 1-800-CALL-NYS.

TENNESSEE
Travelers over 55 can find bargains in the state of Tennessee every September, generally from Labor Day to the end of the month. Sponsored by the Department of Tourist Development, a program called The Senior Class gives you discounts of at least 10 percent on hotels and motels, attractions, restaurants, retail shops, campgrounds, state parks.
For information: For a booklet listing all of the participating businesses, contact The Senior Class, Tennessee Department of Tourist Development, PO Box 23170, Nashville, TN 37202; 615-741-2158.

UTAH
The Silver Card issued by Park City is a summer program of discounts in this old mining town that's known for its great ski mountains. About 40 restaurants and retailers participate in giving older visitors discounts on their wares. To go along with the shopping and eating possibilities, Park City also presents a whole schedule of activities designed especially for the mature crowd.
For information: Park City Area Visitors Bureau, 528 Main St., Park City, UT 84060; 1-800-453-1360 or 801-649-6100.

VERMONT

Vermont's residents over 60 can purchase a Green Mountain Passport for $2 from their own town clerk. It is good for a lifetime and entitles them to free day-use admission at any Vermont State Park and its programs. Other benefits include discounts on concerts, restaurant meals, prescriptions, etc.

VIRGINIA

Williamsburg makes September a special season for people over 55, with more than 80 local businesses offering special discounts and rates (up to 25 percent off) at hotels, motels, guest homes, sight-seeing attractions, restaurants, campgrounds, shops, and the like.

Everybody goes here primarily to visit 18th-century Colonial Williamsburg, Busch Gardens, the historic villages of Jamestown and Yorktown, and the James River Plantations, but there are many other fascinating places, all of them discounted in September. In addition, special events are planned for every day of the month: arts and crafts fairs, concerts, jazz ensembles, plays, tours, hot-air balloon demonstrations, a Scottish festival, lectures.

Your driver's license will do as ID.

For information: Williamsburg Area Tourism and Conference Bureau, PO Box GB, 901 Richmond Rd., Williamsburg, VA 23187; 1-800-368-6511 (in Virginia, 804-253-0192).

WASHINGTON, DC

The Golden Washingtonian Club is a discount program in the nation's capital for people over 60. With proof of age, both residents and visitors can get discounts from about 1,500 merchants listed in a directory called *Gold Mine*, which is free at many hotels or at the Washington Tourist Information Center. More than 70 hotels offer 10 to 40 percent off regular rates, 80 restaurants take 5 to 20 percent off meals, and many retail stores take 5 to 25 percent off purchases.

By the way, remember the Metro System Family/ Tourist Pass in Washington, DC. For $5, this gives up to four people unlimited travel on Metrobus and Metrorail for an entire day (on Saturday, Sunday, and federal holidays).

For information: For a copy of *Gold Mine*, contact Washington Tourist Information Center, 1400 Pennsylvania Ave., NW, Washington, DC 20005; 202-466-GOLD (9:00 A.M. to 5:00 P.M.). If the Metro System Family/Tourist Pass isn't available in your hotel, call 202-637-7000 (6:00 A.M. to 11:30 P.M., seven days a week).

WEST VIRGINIA

Everybody who turns 60 in West Virginia gets a Golden Mountaineer Discount Card, which entitles the bearer to discounts from more than 3,500 participating merchants and professionals in the state and a few outside of it. If you don't receive a card automatically, you may apply for one. Flash it wherever you go and save a bundle.

For information: Call 1-800-642-3671 (in Charleston, 304-348-3317).

Chapter Thirteen
Good Deals for Good Sports

Real sports never give up their sneakers. If you've been a physically active sort all your life, you're certainly not going to be a couch potato now. Especially since you've probably got more time, energy, and maybe funds than you ever had before to enjoy athletic activities and since you may now take advantage of some enticing special privileges and adventures.

The choices outlined here are not for people whose interest in sports is limited to slouching in comfortable armchairs in front of television sets and watching a football game, or settling down on a hard bench in a stadium with a can of beer, yelling, "Come on, team!" They are for peppy people who do the running themselves.

SPORTING GROUPS

NATIONAL SENIOR SPORTS ASSOCIATION

This nonprofit organization has worthy objectives, such as helping you, a sportive person who is over 50, meet new friends and "maintain and improve physical and emotional health through active sports participation."

The NSSA organizes recreational and competitive tournaments in golf, tennis, bowling, skiing, and fishing, at resorts around the country, and arranges sports-oriented trips abroad at special group rates. Last year, for example, there were NSSA events in Bermuda, Las Vegas, Myrtle Beach, Hawaii, Ireland, and Palm Springs, among other choice spots.

Membership—which costs $15 for one year, $40 for three years, $150 for life—entitles you to participate in the sports events and trips and also:

▶ Get discounts on sports equipment, apparel, publications, and leisure products

▶ Travel overseas to play golf or tennis at international resorts

▶ Receive a discount on membership in The Golf Card, which entitles you to play twice on more than 1,200 courses in the US and abroad with no greens fees, and a free subscription to *Golf Traveler* magazine (see details later in this chapter, under "What's Going for Golfers")

▶ Receive a monthly newsletter

▶ Participate in the organization's Vacation Home Exchange program

▶ Enter contests and buy sports books at discounts

▶ Send for names and addresses of members so you can get together for a friendly match when you're traveling on your own

▶ Get a discount for Med-Alert emergency medical system

▶ Receive a discount if you join the golfers' St. Andrews Handicap system

For information: NSSA, 317 Cameron St., Alexandria, VA 22314; 703-549-6711.

OUTDOOR ADVENTURES FOR WOMEN OVER 40
Any reader of this book is certainly over 40 and therefore qualifies, if female, for the trips organized by Outdoor Vacations for Women Over 40. Founded in 1983 by Marion Stoddart, an avid outdoorswoman and conservationist who didn't want to hike, bike, camp out, ski, raft, and canoe with women half her age, this organiza-

tion attracts physically fit adventurers whose ages, to date, have ranged up to 81.

Ms. Stoddart's surveys have found that a little more than half of the participants in her adventure trips are married; about half are employed; the other half are homemakers, retirees, or volunteers. They come from all over the country, though most are from New England, are in good condition, and rate themselves as beginners or intermediates in the activity they're signing up for. They all love the outdoors, or they wouldn't be there.

The trips are led by trained guides and include instruction, lodging, food, transportation. When you're not camping out in tents or under the stars, you'll be staying in first-rate accommodations.

Previous adventures have included two weeks of biking through the Loire Valley in France, 10 days of hiking and rafting in the Southwest's national parks, a canoe trip in Vermont, rafting in Yellowstone. There are also day trips out of the Boston area, doing such things as animal tracking, orienteering, hiking, and canoeing.

For information: Outdoor Vacations for Women, PO Box 200, Groton, MA 01450; 617-448-3331.

THE OVER THE HILL GANG
This international club for energetic people on the far side of 50 began as a ski club (three former Colorado ski instructors were looking for company on the slopes; see Chapter 14), but its members can now be found participating in all kinds of athletic endeavors. Its literature states that it is "an organization for active, fun-loving,

adventurous, enthusiastic, young-thinking persons. The only catch is, you have to be 50 or over to join." (Spouses may be younger, however.) You don't have to be a superjock to be a member, but you do have to like action.

Right now, the club has about 1,000 members and 15 Gangs (chapters) coast to coast (Chicago, Cleveland, Denver, Eastern, Grand Junction, Houston, Los Angeles, Orange County, Miami, New England, Reno, St. Louis, San Diego, Southern California, Texarkana). When there's no Gang in your vicinity, you may become a member at large and join in any of the goings-on. These include ski trips, scuba diving, hiking, vacation trips, camping and fishing, ballooning, surfing, canoeing, whatever. Each Gang decides on its own activities. Just plain travel is on the agenda too (see Chapter 3).

The annual fee ($50 single, $80 per couple for a local Gang membership; $25 and $40 for membership at large) gives you a bimonthly newsmagazine, discounts, and a chance to join the fun.

For information: Over the Hill Gang International, 13791 E. Rice Pl., Aurora, CO 80015; 303-699-6404.

BONUSES FOR BIKERS

Biking is becoming one of America's most popular sports, and people who never dreamed they could go much farther than around the block are now pedaling up to 150 miles in a day. That includes over-the-hill bikers beyond 50 as well as youngsters of 16, 39, or 47. In fact, some tours and clubs in the U.S. and Canada are designed especially for over-50s.

AMERICAN YOUTH HOSTEL BIKE TOURS

Although almost every organized biking tour would be delighted to have you along as long as you are fairly adept at pedaling, there's one outfit that's actively looking for you. That's American Youth Hostels, which despite its name offers bike trips—among other adventure trips (see Chapter 3)—specifically for people over 50. That doesn't mean, of course, that you're not also invited to pedal along on any other adult AYH tour.

You'll stay at hostels that offer simple dormitory-style accommodations, eat local food, and meet people who enjoy doing the same kinds of things you like to do. Trips are limited to groups of 10; all are escorted by trained leaders and are astonishingly inexpensive.

Recent trips offered by AYH exclusively for the mature crowd include cycling in Hawaii and Europe, in New England during the foliage season, and along the Wisconsin Bikeway.

AYH membership, which is required, costs $20 per year unless you're over 60, in which case it's only $10. **For information:** AYH, Dept 855, PO Box 37613, Washington, DC 20013-7613; 202-783-6161.

BICYCLE TOURING FOR WOMEN ONLY

The same agency mentioned earlier, Outdoor Vacations for Women over 40, includes bike trips among its active offerings. Last year, there was a day trip in southern New Hampshire and Massachusetts, a weekend of biking and walking on Cape Cod, another on Martha's Vineyard and Nantucket, a two-week adventure on bicycles in the Loire Valley in France, a combination ca-

noe-and-bike trip in Vermont, and a weekend on Block Island in Long Island Sound.
For information: Outdoor Vacations for Women, PO Box 200, Groton, MA 01450; 617-448-3331

THE CROSS CANADA CYCLE TOUR SOCIETY
This club was formed in 1982 by a group of "senior cyclists," ranging from about 60 to 75, who biked several thousand miles across Canada in 100 days. Since then, the club has sponsored many cycling trips for all ages and gets local members out for 30- to 50-mile rides twice a week. On the long trips, bikers camp out and make many miles a day. Says the society, "Our aim is to stay alive as long as possible," a worthy goal. Membership costs $20 per year single or $30 per family; most members live in British Columbia.
For information: The Cross Canada Cycle Tour Society, 1200 Hornby St., Vancouver, BC, Canada V6Z 2E2.

THE ONTARIO MASTERS CYCLING ASSOCIATION
A biking club that has members from all over the Canadian province of Ontario, all of them over 40 and some of them into their high 70s. It is primarily a racing club and organizes 12 events a year within the province, including time trials of 40 and 80 kilometers as well as pursuit and road races of 60 kilometers.

But the club also organizes bike tours for ordinary nonracing persons of both sexes. And you don't even have to be a formal member to join them—just show up at the start and ride. Among its other enticements, there are social get-togethers, a monthly newsletter listing upcoming events, and tips on buying good bikes and finding good meals en route.

For information: Ontario Masters Cycling Association, RR #3, Caledon East, ON, Canada, L0N 1E0 416-880-5136

BICYCLE RACING

Now we're leaving recreational pedaling behind and getting into really serious stuff. So, unless you're a dedicated racer who's in terrific shape, feel free to skip this section.

The United States Cycling Federation, part of the U.S. Olympic Committee, is a racing organization that conducts races for members between the ages of 9 and 89. It's composed of about 800 member clubs throughout the country that promote activities for beginners and run their own races for the more experienced.

Participants in the events must be USCF-licensed riders (this requires a license fee of $32, a completed form, and proof of citizenship and age). Anybody can join. Everyone starts in the entry-level category, then is upgraded appropriately. Riders over the age of 30 are divided into five-year incremental classes and compete against peers. Women do not race against men but form their own groups.

Members receive a monthly publication that lists the upcoming events. The clubs and local bike shops also can provide information about races.

For information: USCF, 1750 E. Boulder St., Colorado Springs, CO 80909; 303-578-4581.

MORE TIPS FOR BICYCLISTS
The *Tourfinder*, a guide to more than 150 operators who run bicycle tours in the United States and around the world, is available from the League of American Wheelmen. It gives locations, miles covered per day, level of difficulty, prices, accommodations, tour dates, and other information.
For information: League of American Wheelmen, 6707 Whitestone Rd., #209, Baltimore, MD 21207.

TENNIS ANYONE?

An estimated four million of the nation's tennis players are over 50, with the number increasing every year as more of us decide to forgo rocking chairs for a few fast sets on the courts. You need only a court, a racquet, a can of balls, and an opponent to play tennis, but, if you'd like to be competitive or sociable, you may want to get into some senior tournaments.

UNITED STATES TENNIS ASSOCIATION
The USTA offers a wide variety of tournaments for players over the advanced age of 35, at both local and national levels. To participate, you must be a member ($20 per year). When you join, you will become an automatic member of a regional section, receive periodic schedules of USTA-sponsored tournaments and events in your area for which you can sign up, get a discount on tennis books and publications, and receive a monthly newsletter and a free subscription to *World Tennis* magazine.

In the schedule of tournaments, you'll find competi-

tions listed for specific five-year age groups: for men from 35 to 80-plus and for women from 35 to 70-plus. There are also self-rated tournaments that match you up with people of all ages who play at your level. If you feel you're good enough to compete, send for an application and sign up. There is usually a modest fee.
For information: USTA, 729 Alexander Rd., Princeton, NJ 08540; 609-452-2580.

SENIOR NATIONAL CHAMPIONSHIPS
Also sponsored by the USTA are these tournaments for very serious senior players, who are divided into divisions by gender and age. There are four national tournaments per age group—ages 35 to 75 for women and 35 to 85 for men. Singles, doubles, and mixed doubles tournaments are held on four kinds of surfaces—indoor, grass, clay, and hard courts—at facilities throughout the United States. Added attractions: father-son and mother-daughter doubles events.
For information: USTA Seniors Dept., 1212 Ave. of the Americas, New York, NY 10036; 212-302-3322.

SUPER-SENIOR TENNIS
This group, which has been described as "an affinity group" or a fraternity of male players who compete in the USTA tournaments, promotes tennis for men from 55 to 85 (or more) and arranges a series of tennis events for them in warm places like Florida during the off-season.

"Our members like to compete and to win," says a spokesperson. "Our constant aim is more tournaments for players in the USTA age divisions for men 55 and over. . . . Super Senior tennis players are the last true amateurs in the sport. No one gets paid to play in a tournament, no one receives travel expenses, and we discourage prize money tournaments."

In return for your tax-deductible contribution of $12 a year, you receive a membership card and a bimonthly newsletter that lists tournament dates and results and other matters of interest.

For information: Super-Senior Tennis, PO Box 5165, Charlottesville, VA 22905.

TENNIS VACATIONS

All American Sports offers tennis vacations at luxurious resorts in a variety of interesting locations, ranging from Hawaii to Vermont, Puerto Rico, Mexico, Massachusetts, California, and Arizona. What's more, there are special "40's Plus Weeks" for midlife folks and special weeks for "Seniors," which means from about 60 upward. And, as an added incentive, some of the resorts offer a 10 percent discount on their 40's Plus and Senior Weeks. Check this out before you decide where to go.

When you're on one of the tennis vacations, you'll get an evaluation of your current level of play, many hours of instruction, practice, videotape playbacks, strategy sessions, and plenty of playing time in both singles and doubles. You may choose a heavy tennis program or a lighter schedule on the courts that leaves more time for other resort activities. Nonplaying companions may go along with you and need never set foot on the courts if they so choose, taking advantage of the resort's other offerings.

To make sure you come away a better tennis player than you went in, there is "guaranteed improvement." If you feel you haven't improved your game during this stay, you will be given a certificate entitling you to a free tennis program (this does not include accommodations) at any of the resorts within six months.

For information: All American Sports, 45 Kensico Dr., Mt. Kisco, NY 10549; 1-800-223-2442 (in New York State, 914-666-0096).

VAN DER MEER TENNIS CENTER

This center on the resort island of Hilton Head has initiated a Seniors Clinic for all-skill-level players 45 and older. Held in September, the five-day clinic emphasizes doubles tactics, anticipation, and stroke production, and includes 25 hours of instruction plus a personalized evaluation by Dennis Van der Meer. Current cost is $275 with accommodations for only $10 per person per night.

For information: Van der Meer Tennis Center, PO Box 5902, Hilton Head Island, SC 29938-5902; 1-800-845-6138 (in South Carolina, 803-785-9602).

MORE TENNIS VACATIONS

If playing tennis is an essential part of a vacation for you, check out the offerings of the National Senior Sports Association and the Over the Hill Gang (see the beginning of this chapter). These groups organize tennis-oriented trips.

WHAT'S GOING FOR GOLFERS

GREENS FEES

Most municipal and many private golf courses give senior golfers (usually those over 65) a discount off the regular greens fees. Take your identification with you and always make inquiries before you play.

THE GOLF CARD

This card, designed especially for senior golfers with lots of time to play on every possible golf course, costs $65 a year for a single membership or $99 for a couple (NSSA members get a $10 discount). It entitles you to play two complimentary 18-hole rounds at each of about 1,700 member golf courses throughout the world.

You'll also receive the bimonthly *Golf Traveler* magazine, which contains a directory and guide to the courses and resorts that participate and a travel atlas to help you find them.

Added attraction: Discounts at 350 resorts when you book golf travel packages.

There is no age minimum for joining this group, but just to give you an idea of its membership: the average member is 61 and has played golf for 24 years, plays 81 rounds a year, travels 11 weeks a year, travels with a spouse, and plans golf as part of his or her leisure travel.

For information: The Golf Card, 1137 E. 2100 South, PO Box 6439, Salt Lake City, UT 81406; (1-800-453-4260; in Utah, 801-486-9391; in Canada, 1-800-321-8269).

GOLFING VACATIONS

The National Senior Sports Association (see the beginning of this chapter) organizes many golfing vacations for its members at courses and resorts all over the country and abroad. Membership gets you a discount on The Golf Card too.

THE MATURE OUTLOOK GOLF TOURNAMENT

An annual event held in the month of February in Tucson and open to members of Mature Outlook (see Chapter 19), it is managed by the Pacific Amateur Golf Association and is a good deal. The whole package cost $395 for golfers ($305 for nongolfers) in 1987 and included greens fees, a shared cart for three tournament rounds, four nights at the Doubletree Hotel, a cocktail party, and a farewell awards dinner.

For information: Mature Outlook Golf Tournament, PO Box 1214, Glenview, IL 60025.

SWIMMING FOR FUN AND FITNESS

Swimming, a great way to get exercise and stay in shape, is, for most of us, simply a matter of jumping into the nearest lake or pool and butterflying around, maybe doing a few laps. But if you'd like to be organized about it, you'll find that many Ys and other pool operators have special swim classes or meets for adults. Or you can get really serious and join the Masters Swimmers.

U.S. MASTERS SWIMMING

Originally an organization for young competitive swimmers fresh out of college looking for people to race against, today the Masters is a group that is about 80 percent recreational swimmers, many of whom are over 50. Members get swimming insurance and receive a national newsletter and a magazine that offer information about places to swim, groups to swim with, tips on techniques, and the like. There are 54 local associations across the United States for you to hook up with and several weekend or week-long swim camps to consider.

If you're into competition, at whatever age or level of ability, you may participate in local, regional, and even national meets. Competitors are grouped in heats according to their times, regardless of age or sex. But results are tabulated separately for men and women and in five-year age groups right through 90-plus.

For information: USMS National Office, 5 Piggott Ln., Avon, CT 06001; 203-677-9464.

GETTING INTO THE NATIONAL GAMES

U.S. NATIONAL SENIOR OLYMPICS

Inaugurated at Washington University in St. Louis in the summer of 1987, these Olympic games aim to be a biannual event—which makes the next one in 1989. Regional Senior Olympic games have been around for over 15 years, but 1987 was the first time a national competition had ever been staged for older athletes who want to win medals for their prowess. For six days, qualified athletes from all over the country competed in 11 sports.

To qualify for the more than 400 separate events—in track and field, swimming, cycling, golf, tennis, bowling, volleyball, horseshoes, archery, 10-kilometer run, and table tennis—athletes 55 and up must have competed first at sanctioned state and regional Senior Olympics across the country. The events were organized for men and women in five-year age brackets from 55 to 80-plus.

If you want to be ready to go for the next senior games, get the ground rules from your local Senior Olympics organization or the national group.

For information: U.S. National Senior Olympics, 222 S. Central, Suite 505, St. Louis, MO 63105; 314-726-4550.

STATE SENIOR GAMES

Many states hold their own senior games once a year or so and send their best competitors to national events. If you don't find your state among those listed here, that doesn't mean there's no program in your area—many are sponsored by counties, cities, even local agencies and colleges. Check with your local Department of Recreation to see what's going on near you or look in your *Silver Pages* directory (see Chapter 17). You don't have to be a serious competitor to enter the state or local games but merely ready to enjoy yourself. So what if you don't go home with a medal? At the very least, you'll meet other peppy people and have a lot of laughs.

CALIFORNIA
The Southern California Regional Senior Olympics is sponsored by the city of Palm Springs. The first games in 1987 were held over three days and included anyone 55 to 80 (one female swimming contestant was 89) competing in rodeo, ice skating, free-throw shooting, rope skipping, and basketball, as well as all the other sports that could lead to participation in the National Senior Olympics.
For information: Southern California Regional Senior Olympics, Community Services Dept., PO Box 1786, Palm Springs, CA 92263; 619-323-8272.

COLORADO
The Rocky Mountain Senior Games, held in both the summer and the winter, recently celebrated its 10th anniversary. The event is open to residents of Colorado and Wyoming who are 55 and over, with a registration fee of $10. The three-day summer games are held at the University of Northern Colorado in Greeley, Colorado, where you'll pay $12 a night for lodging, and include such events as track and field, swimming, tennis, basketball, bowling, biking, bowling—plus a considerable number of training clinics, workshops, banquets, and dances.
For information: Rocky Mountain Senior Games, 2604 S. Pennsylvania, Denver, CO 80210; 303-777-0471.

The Winter Senior Games, featuring downhill skiing, cross-country skiing, speed and figure skating, a biathlon, and a snowshoeing competition, are usually held in February at a Colorado Ski resort. The registration fee of $10 allows you to participate in as many events as you wish.

For information: Phyllis Hammond, Blue Cross/Blue Shield of Colorado, 700 Broadway, Denver, CO 80273; 303-831-2216.

CONNECTICUT

The Connecticut Senior Olympics includes not only competitive sport events but also a mini-health fair and physical fitness activities. Connecticut residents and those from neighboring states who are 55-plus converge on the University of Bridgeport on the first Saturday in June for a day of events such as the 5,000-meter run, the 100-yard dash, a mile run, the long jump, diving, bocci, and tennis. There is no entrance fee.

For information: Write to Connecticut Senior Olympics, Harvey Hubbell Gymnasium, University of Bridgeport, Bridgeport, CT 06601.

FLORIDA

The Golden Age Games in Sanford are the biggest and the oldest Senior Games in the country. Held annually in November, they go on for a week and include plenty of competitions, ceremonies, social events, and entertainments. If you are over 55, you are eligible to participate regardless of residency. In other words, you needn't be a Florida resident to compete for the gold, silver, and bronze medals in such sports as basketball, biking, bowling, canoeing, checkers, diving, dance, swimming, tennis, triathlon, track and field, canasta, and croquet. There is a small entry fee for each event.

For information: The Greater Sanford Chamber of

Commerce, PO Drawer CC, Sanford, FL 32772-0868; 305-322-2212.

MICHIGAN
Michigan Senior Olympics, a one-day happening open to people over 55, is held in August on the campus of Oakland Community College in Farmington Hills. For a $2 registration fee and $1 per closed event (an event that requires registering for it), you get a T-shirt, lunch, and a chance to compete for a medal in athletic events like discus throwing, 100-yard dash, diving, and cycling. You can also take home ribbons for your superior cookies, cakes, or breads or your prowess at checkers, arts and crafts, and dancing.
For information: Michigan Senior Olympics, O.P.C., 312 Woodward, Rochester, MI 48063; 313-656-1403.

MISSOURI
The St. Louis Senior Olympics has become an institution in Missouri by now. A four-day event that is open to anyone who lives anywhere and is 55 years old, it costs a nominal amount and is action-oriented. No knitting contests here—only energetic events such as bicycle races, 200-meter races, standing long jumps, tennis singles and doubles, and swimming.
For information: Senior Olympics, JCAA, 2 Millstone Campus, St. Louis, MO 63146.

MONTANA
The Big Sky State Games are held each July in Billings, again for people over 55.
For information: The Big Sky Games, PO Box 2318, Billings, MT 59101.

NEW YORK

New York Senior Games for state residents over the age of 55 are usually held on a state college campus over a weekend in the spring. Competition is divided into age categories starting with 55 to 59 and going up to 80-plus with activities ranging from archery and badminton to cycling, billiards, and volleyball. Also included are a dinner with entertainment and dancing, workshops, and clinics—all for a modest fee.

For information: New York Senior Games, State Parks, Agency 1, 12th Fl., Albany, NY 12238; 518-474-2324.

NORTH CAROLINA

After local games held all over the state, the winners of the North Carolina Senior Games travel to Raleigh for the state finals and/or to the national games. Every sport from billiards to spin casting to track is on the agenda.

For information: North Carolina Senior Games, PO Box 33590, Raleigh, NC 27606; 919-851-5456.

PENNSYLVANIA

The Pennsylvania Senior Games "combines sports, recreation, and entertainment with fellowship." You can get some of each if you are a Pennsylvania resident who is 55 or older. The games are held over four days at a university campus where you can get lodging and three meals a day for a remarkably low fee ($20 a day at this writing). If you prefer to stay in a motel, you'll get a

senior discount. The registration fee is $10 for partici-
pants and $8 for spectators.
For information: Pennsylvania Senior Games, 231
State St., Harrisburg, PA 17101-1195.

VERMONT
The Green Mountain Senior Games in Poultney, whose
major sponsor is Killington Ski Area, require you to be
a Vermont resident who is over 55 and an amateur at
your sport. For a $5 registration fee, you play, eat
lunch, and have fun. Competitive events—organized in
age groups of 55 to 62, 63 to 70, and 71 and over—
include everything from golf and tennis to swimming,
darts, horseshoes, walking, running, table tennis, bowling, croquet, softball and shuffleboard. Just for fun,
there are folk and square dancing, volleyball, walking,
free swims. The games are held in the early fall.
For information: Green Mountain Senior Games, PO
Box 1660, Station A, Rutland, VT 05701.

VIRGINIA
Virginia Golden Olympics is a four-day happening in
the spring, this one at Lynchburg College, where athletes compete to qualify for the U.S. National Senior
Olympics—or just for the fun of it. The event combines
social events and entertainment with sports events. The
fees are low, lodging and meals are cheap, and the
sporting events are many. Some of the more novel competitions include jump rope, miniature golf, riflery,
and Frisbee throws along with the usual swimming,

tennis, running, and the like, for various age groups from 55 to 85-plus.

For information: Golden Olympics, PO Box 2774, Lynchburg, VA 24501; 804-847-1640.

WASHINGTON

A truly athletic happening, the Seattle Senior Sports Festival is a Regional Qualifying Event for the national games and involves only serious sports including track and field, tennis, lawn bowling, pickleball, swimming, table tennis, and softball. Entry fee is $8 for as many sports as you'd like to enter. You are eligible if you are 55 or over and are an amateur in your chosen sport.

For information: Senior Sports Festival, 100 Dexter Ave. North, Seattle, WA 98109-5199; 206-625-2981.

EVENTS FOR RAPID RUNNERS

MASTERS TRACK & FIELD AND ROAD RACES

Masters are men and women 30 and over who participate in organized track and field meets and road races. There are no qualifications to join. "About all you need is a pair of shorts, a pair of shoes, and an occasional entry fee if you decide to compete in a meet or race," says *National Masters News*, a monthly newspaper and the main source of information about events, providing results, schedules, and local information for each region of the country. "Masters competition is divided into 5- or 10-year age groups for men and women. Every event from the 100-yard dash to the shot put to the marathon is available."

If you want to compete after working out on your own

or in a club, there are many meets and races with prizes awarded by age categories. For most of them, you simply show up at the right time and place, register, and participate, although you may wish to sign up in advance.

When you're really experienced, you travel to regional, national, and international competitions, where you'll pay your own expenses and compete as an individual. "The championship events are open to everyone," says long-distance running committee chairman Bob Boal.

For information: Masters Long Distance Running, TAC/USA, 4261 S. 184th St., Seattle, WA 98188. To subscribe to the monthly newspaper, write to *National Masters News*, PO Box 5185, Pasadena, CA 91107.

Chapter Fourteen
Adventures on Skis

OVER THE TOP ON TWO NARROW BOARDS

Downhill skiing is one sport you'd think would appeal only to less mature, less wise, less breakable people. On the contrary, there is an astounding number of ardent over-50 skiers who would much rather glide down mountains than sit around waiting for springtime. In fact, many of us ski more than ever now that we're older because we can go midweek, when the crowds are thinner. And many of us are taking up the sport for the first time. Ski schools all over the United States and Canada are reporting an increase of older students in beginner classes.

The truth is, skiing is one sport you're never too old to learn or to practice. Once you get the hang of it, you can ski at your own speed, choosing the terrain, the difficulty level, and the challenge. You can swoop down cliffs through narrow icy passes or wend your way down gentle slopes in a more leisurely fashion, aided by the new improved skis and boots, clearly marked and carefully groomed trails, and those newfangled lifts that take all the work out of getting up the mountain.

Besides, ski resorts are falling all over themselves to lure older skiers to their slopes, offering discounts, free passes, and other engaging incentives. Many over-50 groups sponsor ski activities as well.

CLUBS FOR MATURE SKIERS

THE OVER THE HILL GANG

As we have noted, this group originated with a group of older skiers who wanted companionship on the slopes, and skiing is still its main emphasis. In fact, its motto is "Once you're over the hill, you pick up speed!"

If you've hit 50, you are eligible to join (your spouse may be younger) and set forth on ski adventures—both downhill and cross-country—in this country and abroad. Members get discounts on lifts and rentals and sometimes are the recipients of free group guides and special lift line privileges. People who have never put on a pair of ski boots or haven't tried them in years can take advantage of refresher clinics or group lessons arranged by the club.

And when the ski season ends, you can join the Gang for a bike trip, a party, maybe rafting or ballooning or a sailing trip in the Caribbean. This club, with an age range of 50 to 94 and an average age of 58, is definitely out for fun.

Every year the club organizes a Senior Ski Week in the Rockies or Europe, a package deal that includes accommodations, parties, food, and lift tickets, sometimes lessons. And many members participate in a week of skiing at five different resorts around Lake Tahoe.

The local Gangs also run their own ski trips both in their own vicinities and elsewhere in the world, and all members everywhere are invited to go along. Often there are certain days of the week that the Gangs gather, meeting at a ski area's base lodge and dividing into groups with their own member guides. They rally at reserved spots for lunch, ski some more, then get together for après-ski gatherings and a bit of bragging.

Membership in a local Gang costs $50 ($80 for a couple). If there's no Gang in your vicinity, you may join the national club as an at-large member for $25 ($40

per couple). A quarterly newsletter is part of the deal.
For information: Over the Hill Gang International,
13791 E. Rice Pl., Aurora, CO 80015; 303-699-6404.

70+ SKI CLUB

You have to prove you are 70 before you're invited to
join this club, which now has about 3,000 members in
their 70s and 80s and a few in their 90s, all of them
active downhill skiers. The club meets at various ski
areas—usually in New York or New England—for
races, companionship, and partying and organizes big
trips in the United States and Europe.

Lloyd T. Lambert, a former ski writer who was born
in 1901, founded the 70+ Ski Club in 1977 with 34
members. One purpose was to make skiing less expensive for older people on limited retirement incomes. He
urged ski areas to let members ski free or at discounts,
and his campaign worked. Today most ski areas give us
offers we can't refuse. Says Lambert, "We provide in-
spiration to the 40-year-olds who are about to give up
the sport because they think they're getting feeble."

Hunter Mountain in New York's Catskills hosts the
club's annual one-day meeting early in March every
year. This is when the annual 70+ Ski Races are held,
an event so popular that the contestants are divided
into three categories—men 70 to 80, women 70 to 80,
and everyone over 80. There are serious slalom races as
well as "fun" races with awards for the winners presented at a gala party at the lodge.

Most gatherings of the members take place at ski
areas in New England and feature special races and
special events, but there are always a couple of week-

long ventures to the Alps and the Rockies. And the club has members all over the United States and Canada, even some in Europe.

Club members pay only $5—for life. Proof of your date of birth is required with your application, and you must not apply more than two weeks before your 70th birthday! You'll receive a 70+ Ski Club patch, a membership card, a newsletter, and a list of ski areas throughout the country where you can ski free or at a discount. You can also get a list of members for an additional fee so you can arrange your own companionship if you wish.

For information: Lloyd T. Lambert, 70+ Ski Club, 104 Eastside Dr., Ballston Lake, NY 12019; 518-399-5458.

BROMLEY SENIOR SKIERS CLUB

Free membership in this Bromley Mountain, Vermont, club provides skiers over 65 with half-price lift tickets or a half-price season pass, discounts on lift-lesson-equipment packages for family members, and preferred parking midweek. Report to Customer Service with your ID for a club card and a parking permit.

For information: Vermont Ski Areas Association, Box 368, Montpelier, VT 05602.

STRATTON SENIOR SKIERS ASSOCIATION

Join this Stratton Mountain (Vermont) group for a $10 annual fee. Members 62 through 69 may ski for half price, and those over 70 may ski free. All may also participate in a special Senior Day each spring that includes races and a reception.

For information: Vermont Ski Areas Association, Box 368, Montpelier, VT 05602.

WATERVILLE VALLEY SILVER STREAKS

The Silver Streaks of Waterville Valley, New Hampshire, are members of a club for skiers who have reached their 55th birthday (and spouses at any age). Silver Streakers buy a $20 lift ticket ($5 off regular midweek price) the first time they ski. On subsequent nonholiday midweek visits, the lift ticket is reduced $2 each time until it reaches $10, the price paid the rest of the season. On Tuesdays and Wednesdays, you get even more: reserved parking, free coffee and donuts, warm-up runs with the ski-school instructors, and Silver Streak NASTAR races. Your card will also entitle you to reduced prices on rentals and class lessons.

For beginners over 55, the resort offers a learn-to-ski package with lifts, ski lesson, and rental equipment, all for $20 a day.

Members of the 70+ Ski Club—and any other intrepid skiers over 70—ski free.

For information: Silver Streaks, Waterville Valley Resort, Waterville Valley, NH 03215; 603-236-8311.

THE WILD OLD BUNCH

This merry band of senior skiers who navigate the steep slopes of Alta in Utah is an informal bunch of men and women from Utah and many other states who ski together for fun, welcoming anybody who wants to join them. There are no rules, no designated leaders, no lessons, no regular meetings, and no age restrictions, though most members are well past 50, retired business or professional people. Somewhere between 50 and 100 avid skiers now wear the patch.

The group grows haphazardly as members pick up any stray skiers they find on the slopes, showing them their mountain and passing along their enthusiasm for the steeper trails and the off-trail skiing in Alta's famous powder. Says a spokesperson, Rush Spedden, "If you visit Alta and would like to join in some of the old-fashioned camaraderie of skiing, just look for any of us on the slopes or on the deck of the mid-mountain Alpenglow Inn, where we gather for lunch and tales. Either ski with us or grab a seat for some lively conversation."

Although the bunch isn't sexist, some of the wives "prefer to stay on less difficult slopes or to travel the cross-country trails, so they wear 'Wild Wives' patches."

For information: Look for the Wild Old Bunch on the slopes, or, if absolutely necessary, contact Rush Spedden, 4131 Cumorah Dr., Salt Lake City, UT 84117; 801-278-2283.

MORE DISCOUNTS AND FREEBIES FOR DOWNHILL SKIERS

There's hardly a ski area in the country today that doesn't give mature folks a good deal. Many cut the price of lift tickets in half at age 60, others at 62 or 65, and some stop charging at all when you are 65 or 70.

To give you an idea of what some of the ski areas offer you, here is a short list of possibilities throughout North America. This does not include all areas, of course, so be sure to check out others in locations that interest you. *Always ask* if there is a senior discount before buying your lift ticket.

Proof of age will be required in most cases, so remember to take along some identification that includes your date of birth.

BRITISH COLUMBIA
Blackcomb Mountain in Whistler provides a free pass to anyone 65 or older. For a fee of $5, you can receive a Young at Heart season pass that's good on all lifts.

CALIFORNIA
At Mammoth Mountain, there is no charge over 65.
Alpine Meadows is half price over 65, no charge at 70.

COLORADO
Aspen, Snowmass, Buttermilk, Vail, Steamboat, Keystone, Winter Park, Ski Cooper at Leadville, and Copper Mountain are among the areas offering discounted lift tickets, some starting at 62. In many areas, there is no charge over 70. At Ski Cooper, for example, you're entitled to a full-day lift ticket for $5 if you are over 60, and you don't have to pay even that if you've hit 70. Rental equipment is discounted to $8 for a full day and $6 for a half day.

MAINE
Sunday River Ski Resort in Bethel has a White Caps program for skiers 65 and over. You pay $25 for an all-day lift ticket, three hours of instruction, and lunch.

MICHIGAN
At Crystal Mountain in Thompsonville, senior skiers—

55 and older—get a 50 percent discount on all-day lift tickets, valid anytime. The area's Silver Streak Ski Week, also for people 55 and over, is held in midwinter and includes lodging, unlimited skiing, parties, sing-alongs, races, ski clinic, yoga sessions, and more. Both downhill and cross-country skiing here.

NEVADA
Sun Valley and Mt. Rose are half price if you're over 65.

NEW HAMPSHIRE
At Loon Mountain in Lincoln, those 65 to 70 pay a few dollars less than the other skiers for midweek lift tickets and approximately half for season passes, while those above 70 pay not a cent. Also, see page 146 for information about Waterville Valley's ski club.

NEW YORK
At Gore Mountain in North Creek, you get a junior rate throughout the season if you're over 62, and you'll ski free if you're over 70. Every year, the area hosts a special race day for members of the 70+ Ski Club, with fun races, a giant slalom race, a cocktail party, and an awards banquet.

PENNSYLVANIA
Discounted lift tickets are available for Camelback in Tannersville on midweek nonholidays.

UTAH
Park City, Snowbird, and other resorts offer reduced rates for people who have made it past 62.

VERMONT

Vermont's ski areas are old hands at discounts for mature skiers. Among them are the following:

Stratton gives you half-price lift tickets if you are 62 to 69 and doesn't charge at all over 70. More advantages if you join the Stratton Senior Skiers Association (see the beginning of this chapter).

At Bolton Valley, skiers 65 and over receive a 50 percent discount on all lift tickets.

At Okemo Mountain, those 65 to 69 ski at half price, and those over 70 ski free.

For anyone over 65, half price is available at Pico on lift tickets, ski lessons, and equipment rentals. Those over 70 ski free on weekdays and for half price on weekends.

If you're over 65, you get a complimentary season pass to Haystack if you'll be doing a lot of skiing. Otherwise, you're entitled to free day tickets.

Jay Peak offers free lift tickets for skiers 65 and over, and races are organized for 60s and over.

Mt. Mansfield at Stowe offers discounted lift tickets if you're 65 to 69 and free skiing for those over 70.

At Ascutney, those 62 and older are offered a $10 lift ticket that's valid anytime. If you're over 70, it's free.

Suicide Six and the Woodstock Inn offer the Ski Vermont Free package, which is a deal that's not only for senior skiers—it's available to anyone—but it's a good one. Arrive any night Sunday through Thursday and ski free Monday through Friday. Three nights earn a complimentary lesson. Children 14 and under may stay free in the same room with an adult and also get free skiing privileges. The same arrangements apply to cross-country skiing (see details later in this chapter).

Also, see page 145 for information about Bromley's Senior Skiers Club.

VIRGINIA

At Massanutten Mountain in Harrisonburg, those 65 and over pay about two-thirds of the regular rates for lift tickets and ski rentals.

OTHER ALPINE ADVENTURES

THE ASPEN SKIING COMPANY

Aspen has designed a program for skiers over 50 because more than 27 percent of the skiers at Aspen/ Snowmass are in this age group. The Fit for Life/50 Plus program aims to improve fitness as well as skiing skills and is endorsed by the President's Council on Physical Fitness. The package (which is moderately priced and costs even less for participants over 70) is for a midwinter week (any time from early December through mid-February) and includes lodging at the Inn at Aspen; ski instruction on Buttermilk, Snowmass, or Aspen Mountain; ski video and analysis; seminars on nutrition, stress management, and fitness; and races and parties. The whole thing is aimed at improving your fitness, your attitude, your vigor, and your skiing abilities.

For information: Call the Inn at Aspen at 1-800-952-1515 (in Colorado, 1-800-826-4998).

ELDERHOSTEL DOWNHILL SKIING

The Sunday River Inn in Newry, Maine, is the first Elderhostel campus to offer alpine skiing. The week-long programs available several times during the winter include daily skiing and instruction at Sunday River Ski Resort, plus your choice of a number of academic courses. These, like all the other Elderhostel residence courses, are great bargains.

For information: Elderhostel, 80 Boylston St., Suite 400, Boston, MA 02116; 617-426-8056.

DOWNHILL RACES FOR ALL AGES (YOURS INCLUDED)

NASTAR

NASTAR (National Standard Race) is a ski-racing program sponsored by *Ski* magazine for recreational downhill skiers whatever their age, with 5,000 races held in ski areas all over the United States for medals based on age, sex, and handicap. The age divisions that apply to *you* are the following: men and women 50 to 59, women 60 and over, men 60 to 69, and men 70 and over. You may race on your own or as part of a participating ski club.

If you want to join in the fun, ask for the NASTAR Registration Desk at your ski area, fill out the registration card that registers you for the season, pay a fee, and get a souvenir race bib. Each time you race, your day's best handicap will automatically be recorded at the NASTAR Computer Center, where your best three handicaps of the season will be averaged. If you are a winner in your age group (finalists include 10 men and 10 women from each age category), you will be treated to an expense-paid trip to the finals.

For information: NASTAR, PO Box 4580, Aspen, CO 81612; 303-925-7864.

CROSS-COUNTRY SKI ADVENTURES

Many cross-country areas also give senior skiers a break. Always ask about discounts before paying admission.

CROSS-COUNTRY SKI AREAS DIRECTORY

Destinations is a national directory of cross-country ski areas. Regional maps (Northeast, Midwest, Rocky Mountains, West Coast) are also available.

For information: To get the directory, send $2 to Cross Country Ski Areas of America, RD #2, Bolton Rd., Winchester, NH 03451. Send 50¢ for each regional map.

CROSS-COUNTRY VACATIONS FOR WOMEN ONLY

If you're female and 40, you qualify for the ski trips run by Outdoor Vacations for Women over 40, and that should make you very happy. This company offers some pretty exciting adventures and promises you the fellowship of women your own age.

For women living near Groton, Massachusetts, there are one-day cross-country ski clinics designed for beginners and intermediates. A day includes lessons, lunch, and ski touring, all for very little cost. Then there are ski weekends in Vermont where you stay at a cozy inn, take lessons, and ski as far as you want; and last year there were 10 days of skiing in Yellowstone National Park in Wyoming and Big Sky in Montana and a two-week ski vacation in Norway in the spring.

For information: Outdoor Vacations for Women Over 40, PO Box 200, Groton, MA 01450; 617-448-3331.

ELDERHOSTEL

Elderhostel, known for its low-cost learning vacations for people over 60 (and companions who may be younger) at educational institutions (see Chapter 16), has combined cross-country skiing and winter nature exploration since 1978. For instance, at Craftsbury Center in Craftsbury, Vermont, you can ski on a network of trails, explore the countryside, and take courses. At Frost Valley Environmental Education Center in New York's Catskill Mountains, you can ski and learn on 4,500 acres, while at Old Keystone Village in Colorado you'll intersperse courses in ecology and the history of the Rockies with ski touring at 9,200 feet above sea level. At Las Palomas de Taos, New Mexico, you may alternate ski touring with classes on the foods of the Southwest and the arts of Taos.

For information: Elderhostel, 80 Boylston St., Suite 400, Boston, MA 02116; 617-426-8056.

SENIORS ON SNOW

This series of special cross-country ski programs geared to those 50 and over is offered every winter by the Woodstock Inn in Woodstock, Vermont. The programs are designed for adventurous athletic sorts who love snow but aren't into hurtling down mountains. The sessions take place at this deluxe Rockresort in a beautiful New England village filled with 18th-century houses and are available in three-day midweek or weekend packages.

Included in the packages—which are quite reasonably priced—are three nights' lodging, breakfasts and dinners, cross-country ski lessons, equipment, fitness lectures and movies, tours, receptions, and even a picnic. Also included is the use of the inn's other facilities, among which are the fitness center, indoor pool, saunas, indoor tennis courts, and more.

Three of the sessions assume you have had little or no skiing experience and start you off at "square one." The fourth program is designed for intermediate and advanced skiers. You'll take guided ski tours along a 75-kilometer network of mapped and groomed trails through open pastures and woods.

Another good deal offered by the Woodstock Inn—for all ages—is its Ski Vermont Free program. Arrive any night Sunday through Thursday and ski free Monday through Friday either downhill at Suicide Six or cross-country at the Touring Center. Equipment is also free, and a complimentary lesson comes with a three-night stay.

For information: Rockresorts, 30 Rockefeller Plaza, New York, NY 10112; 1-800-223-7637 (in New York State, 1-800-442-8198); or Woodstock Inn & Resort, 14 The Green, Woodstock, VT 05091; 802-457-1100.

WATERVILLE VALLEY

This New Hampshire ski area has started a special cross-country ski package, the Old-Fashioned Winter Getaway, for skiers over 55. This gives you two nights' lodging at the Snowy Owl Inn with continental breakfast, plus two dinners at O'Keefe's Restaurant, a wine and cheese party, a sleigh ride in the White Mountain National Forest, morning stretch classes, access to the Indoor Sports Center, two cross-country classes, unlimited use of 60 kilometers of groomed trails, and a guided tour with a picnic lunch! And it's inexpensive at that.

Cross-country skiers may also join Waterville Valley Silver Streaks (see page 146) if they are over 55 and apply the membership benefits to the resort's 100-kilometer cross-country center.

For information: Waterville Valley Lodging Bureau, Waterville Valley, NH 03215; 1-800-258-8988 or 603-236-8371 (in New Hampshire, 1-800-552-4767).

RACES FOR CROSS-COUNTRY SKIERS

To ski in the international races run every year by the World Masters Cross-Country Ski Association, you must be over 30. The competitions are separated into five-year age classes all the way up to 75+, separated also by gender. Participants from all nations are invited, and each country is allowed one scoring A team per class and any number of nonscoring B teams. The championship races are held once a year, in Austria in 1988, Canada in 1989, and Sweden in 1990.

For information: World Masters Cross-Country Ski Association USA, 332 Iowa Ave., PO Box 718, Hayward, WI 54843; 715-634-4891.

Chapter Fifteen
Back to Summer Camp

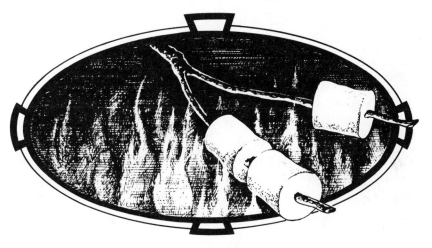

Maybe you thought camp was for kids, but if you are a grown-up person who likes the outdoors, swimming, boating, birds, and arts and crafts and who appreciates fields and forests and star-filled skies, you too can pack your bags and go off to a "sleepaway." Throughout the country, many camps set aside weeks for adult sessions, while others offer adult programs all season long. More and more adults are getting hooked on summer camp, and many wouldn't miss a year.

ELDERHOSTEL

Many of Elderhostel's programs are a combination of camping and college. In this wildly successful low-cost educational program (see Chapter 16 for details), you can spend a week or two camping in remote scenic areas, enjoying all the activities from horseback riding to crafts, boating, campfires, and sleeping under the stars (or in a cabin). As an example, there are Elderhostel weeks at Classroom of the Earth, affiliated with Colvig Silver Camps, in Red Creek Valley near Durango, Colorado. Most Elderhostel weeks are held, however, on college or university campuses in this country and abroad, where you live in a dorm, eat in the college dining rooms, and take courses in subjects that appeal to you.

For information: Elderhostel, 80 Boylston St., Suite 400, Boston, MA 02116; 617-426-8056.

INTERHOSTEL

Sponsored by the University of New Hampshire, Interhostel offers similar arrangements to those of Elderhostel, also inexpensive, but always in foreign countries

and for at least two weeks at a stretch (see pages 167–68 in Chapter 16).
For information: Interhostel, University of New Hampshire, 6 Garrison Ave., Durham, NH 03824; 603-862-1147.

GRANDPARENTS CAMP
Every August, you can take your grandchild/grandchildren to camp with you for a week. Designed to help long-distance grandparents get to know their grandchildren and to allow two generations to spend time together free from the restraints of the kids' parents and the responsibilities of everyday life, the camp is sponsored by the Foundation for Grandparenting. The place is Sagamore Institute, a rustic, rambling, nonprofit conference and outdoor recreation center in Raquette Lake, New York, in the Adirondack Mountains. This place was, in a former life, a Vanderbilt family "great camp."

Mornings, children and grandparents engage in joint activities such as walks, hikes, berry-picking, group games, and nature art. Afternoons, each age group is on its own, free to choose from a variety of recreational activities. Before dinner, grandparents get together for discussions on grandparenting issues, and evening sessions again feature togetherness and include such activities as square dancing, stories, campfires, and sing-alongs.
For information: Sagamore Lodge and Conference Center, Sagamore Rd., Raquette Lake, NY 13436; 315-354-5311; or Foundation for Grandparenting, PO Box 97, Jay, NY 12941; 518-946-2177.

THE SALVATION ARMY

The Salvation Army operates 55 rural camps across the country, most of which have year-round adult sessions. The camps are run by regional divisional headquarters of the Army; thus, each is totally different from the others. Open to anyone, they cost very little.

For information: Contact a local unit of the Salvation Army or write to the national headquarters at 799 Bloomfield Ave., Verona, NJ 07044.

VACATIONS AND
SENIOR CENTERS ASSOCIATION

VASCA is a nonprofit organization that will give you information about camps for people over 55 in the New York area. It represents 17 vacation lodges scattered about New York, New Jersey, Connecticut, and Pennsylvania, most of them for people with an income below a specified level. Some are small rustic wilderness camps, and some are huge sprawling complexes with endless activities. They are sponsored by various nonprofit organizations and foundations, many with religious affiliations, and most are extremely cheap.

For information: VASCA, 275 Seventh Ave., New York, NY 10001; 212-645-6590.

YMCA/YWCA

The Y runs lots of camps, most of them for children, but with special sessions for adults over 50. For example, Westwind on the Pacific is a 500-acre camp owned by the Portland, Oregon, YWCA and located on the coast at the mouth of the Salmon River Estuary. Its senior week, for people over 55, is held every August

and costs about $100 for everything. Camp Cheerio, run by the High Point, North Carolina, YMCA, is in the Appalachian Mountains and sets aside three weeks a year for campers over 50, who live in the same cabins and pursue all the same activities as the kids do during the rest of the summer.
For information: Ask your local Y for information about camps in your area.

CAMPS SPONSORED BY CHURCH GROUPS
There are many camps and summer workshops run by church organizations, too many and too diverse to list here. One source of information is Christian Camping International. This organization offers the *Official Guide to Christian Camps and Conference Centers*, which costs a few dollars.
For information: Christian Camping International, PO Box 646, Wheaton, IL 60189; 312-462-0300.

AUDUBON ECOLOGY CAMPS
Not for over-50s alone, these camps are included here because mature nature freaks will love these natural history programs for adults run by the National Audubon Society. Audubon Ecology Camps are located in Connecticut, Maine, and Wyoming, with sessions varying from 6 to 12 days.
For information: National Audubon Society, 613 Riversville Rd., Greenwich, CT 06831; 203-869-2017.

Chapter Sixteen
Going Back to School After 50

Have you always wanted to learn French, study African birds, examine Eskimo culture, delve into archaeology, international finance, horticulture, the language of whales, or great literature of the 19th century? Now is the time to do it. If you're a typical member of the over-50s generation, you're in good shape, healthy and alert, with the energy and the time to pursue new interests. So why not go back to school and learn all those things you've always wished you knew?

You are welcome as a regular student at just about any institution in the United States and Canada, especially in the continuing-education programs, but many colleges and universities have set up special deals and programs designed to lure older people back to the classroom. Some offer good reductions in tuition (so good indeed that sometimes you may attend classes free) and give credits for life experience. Others have set up programs designed specifically for mature scholars. In some cases, there are whole schools set up just for you.

Going back to class is an excellent way to generate feelings of accomplishment and to exercise the mind—and one of the best ways to make new friends. It doesn't necessarily mean you'll have to turn in term papers or take excruciatingly difficult exams. Sign up for one class a week on flower arranging or Spanish conversation or a once-a-month lecture series on managing your money. Or register as a part-time or full-time student in a traditional university program. Or take a learning vacation on a college campus. Do it *your* way.

THE INSTITUTE OF LIFETIME LEARNING

Part of the many services of the American Association of Retired Persons (see Chapter 20), the Institute of Lifetime Learning acts as a clearinghouse and research center on education for older learners and can be a great help in finding out about educational opportunities. Among its most useful offerings is a booklet, *Tuition Policies in Higher Education for Older Adults*, which tells which traditional colleges and universities throughout the country do or do not offer you free or reduced tuition.

Another booklet, *College Centers for Older Learners*, is a state-by-state listing of learning programs designed specifically for mature students. These range from continuing education to peer-teaching programs. **For information:** Institute of Lifetime Learning, 1909 K St., NW, Washington, DC 20049; 202-662-4895.

CAMPUS STUDY/ TRAVEL PROGRAMS

ELDERHOSTEL

Elderhostel, an educational program for older people who want to expand their horizons, offers some of the world's best bargains. Inspired by European hostels and Scandinavian folk schools, it is a network of about 1,000 schools, colleges, and universities in all 50 states, all 10 Canadian provinces, and more than 35 countries overseas, which offer inexpensive short-term residential learning vacations. To qualify, you must be over 60 (or over 50 to accompany someone who is mature enough to enroll).

You live on a campus for a week or more and take up to three courses chosen from a selection of subjects in the liberal arts and sciences taught by the host institution's faculty. These are not for credit, and there are no exams, grades, or required homework; nor must you have any prerequisite knowledge or degrees.

Each institution hosting Elderhostel programs is different in location, size, academic orientation, and atmosphere, and the courses frequently have a regional flavor. The range of courses stretches toward the infinite, an array of impressive proportions, so you are sure to find some that appeal to you. To name a few recent possibilities: Birds of the Southwest, The History of Country Music, The Rise of Western Civilization, Human Anatomy, Ecology of Alaska, Pollution Alias Self-Destruction, Creative Writing, The Shaker Way of Life, Wines of the World, Vegetarian Garnishes, Appalachian Heritage, the Literature of the Holocaust, and The Art of Weaving.

Most Elderhostel programs are for one week, beginning on a Sunday afternoon and ending the next Saturday morning. You'll sleep in a dormitory. Accommodations vary, ranging from rustic cabins in the Rockies to urban high-rises at city universities. You'll dine on campus food, simple but nourishing, and partake of the school's recreational and cultural resources. The cost for programs in the United States and Canada is remarkably low, usually a little over $200, which covers tuition, room, board, and extracurricular activities. Getting to and from the campus is your responsibility. Many people, incidentally, link Elderhostel weeks, moving from campus to campus for two or three weeks.

The international programs combine morning

classes with afternoon excursions, the campus serving as home base as you study the culture, history, and lore of the land with native instructors. These trips cost more, of course, because they usually last three weeks with stays at three different campuses and include land travel as well as airfare from gateway cities.

There is sure to be an Elderhostel program in a place you've always wanted to visit, giving courses you've always wanted to take, at almost any time of the year.

For information: For a free catalogue and other details; Elderhostel, 80 Boylston St., Suite 400, Boston, MA 02116; 617-426-8056. In Canada: Elderhostel Canada, Corbett House, 29 Prince Arthur Ave., Toronto, Canada M5R 1B2.

INTERHOSTEL

An international study-travel program for peppy people over the age of 50, Interhostel is sponsored by the University of New Hampshire. It offers two-week "educational experiences" at colleges and universities in Europe, China, and Australia. The idea is to stay in one place long enough to learn a lot about it, rather than taking a whirlwind tour. So, if you go, you'll come back well acquainted with the country you're visiting. During your stay, you are introduced to its history, culture, and people through a combination of lectures, field trips, and social activities. Your group—limited to 40 people—will be accompanied by a representative of the University of New Hampshire, just to make sure all goes well. The trips are scheduled from April to October.

Again, your living quarters—"clean and comfortable, though not necessarily fancy"—will be in residence halls. Your meals are usually served cafeteria-style and feature the local food of the region. The cost, which is moderate for what you get, includes two weeks' full room and board, tuition, and ground transportation. Round-trip airfare is the least expensive fare available.

Because Interhostel's adventures impose a rigorous schedule of activities and happenings, the agency discourages people who aren't in good health, full of vim and vigor, and ready to go.

Among the current enticements are two-week trips to various cities in England, the Scottish Highlands, Ireland, Germany, Puerto Rico, Portugal, Sweden, Switzerland, Spain, China, and more, all of which cost around $1,100 plus airfare. Longer adventures to Australia and the Fiji Islands and to China cost a bit more. **For information:** Interhostel, University of New Hampshire, 6 Garrison Ave., Durham, NH 03824; 603-862-1147.

INTERNATIONAL FRIENDSHIP SERVICE

You can go to college in Europe for intensive instruction in a foreign language (even if you are a beginner) pretty much on a shoestring by signing up for this organization's 1- to 12-week summertime seminars abroad. There are no age limitations—you may be anywhere from 16 to 96, and many of the students are nearing the latter. Current programs are centered at universities in Neuchâtel (Switzerland), Heidelberg (Germany), Cannes (France), Santa Margherita Ligure (Italy), and Corte (Corsica).

What you get at the universities are many hours of

French, German, or Italian instruction a week, lodging in student housing or hotel, excursions, tuition, sometimes meals, and other activities. Airfare is not included in the package prices, which are definitely on the moderate side.

For information: International Friendship Service, 22994 El Toro Rd., El Toro, CA 92630; 714-458-8868.

UNIVERSITY VACATIONS (UNIVAC)

Also for students of all ages, Univac puts you up in a comfortable spacious room for sessions of a week to 12 days in April, July, or August, at either of the two oldest university cities in Europe: Oxford or Cambridge in England. Here mornings are spent attending a series of lectures presented by university scholars, with each session concentrating on a specific subject such as Chaucer's England, the Days of King Arthur and Camelot, Medieval Life, Great Castles and Cathedrals, and the England of Henry James and T. S. Eliot. Afternoons are free for excursions or explorations. Again, the costs aren't likely to break the bank.

For information: Oxford-Cambridge Univac, 9602 N.W. 13th St., Miami, FL 33172; 305-591-1736.

PEER LEARNING PROGRAMS

There are currently about 35 learning programs within colleges and universities throughout the country whose basic concept is peer learning and teaching. This means that classes are led by members, rather than paid faculty, who have special expertise in the subject at hand. The study groups take the form of discussion

NEVER-TOO-OLD-TO-LEARN DEPARTMENT

SeniorNet started out at the University of San Francisco as a research project to study the use of computer communication networking by people in the over-49 crowd. But it has developed into a club for learners and users of computers. Members may use the equipment at any of several sites throughout the country or join the network via their own computers, modems, software, and phone lines at home.

As a member of SeniorNet, you can send electronic mail to other members; have access to electronic services, programs, and databases; participate in discussions on specific topics; and take part in on-line conferences with the rest of the membership. A manual tells you how to hook up to the network, and a monthly newsletter keeps you up on the latest developments. A membership directory provides information about the interests, expertise, and backgrounds of the rest of the group, allowing you to choose people you'd like to communicate with.

If you live near a SeniorNet site, you can go there for training, networking, and sociability. There are centers at this writing in San Francisco, Los Angeles, Dallas, Valley City (North Dakota), East Lansing (Michigan), Menlo Park, Colorado Springs, Framingham (Massachusetts), Syracuse (New York), and Falls Church (Virginia). More are in the works.

Annual membership costs $5 and includes the newsletter, the handbook, and a guide that tells you how to connect to the network and make use of its functions. You must pay for your own network time.

For information: SeniorNet, Lone Mountain Campus, Rossi Wing, University of San Francisco, San Francisco, CA 94117-1080; 415-666-6605.

seminars, lectures, workshops, studio classes, or field trips, with the curriculum planned by the members. In some cases, though not all, members must be retired professionals or executives.

There are no tests or grades, though there may be assigned reading or other preparation, and the plan always includes social activities. Students pay an annual membership fee and may take as many courses as they wish. They also receive student status at the university, giving them all of the usual campus privileges, including the use of the library and the swimming pool.

At many of the schools, you may also take one or two regular undergraduate courses each semester as part of your membership, either without charge or at reduced tuition.

THE INSTITUTE FOR RETIRED PROFESSIONALS

At the New School for Social Research in New York, established in 1962, this was the first such program. As the granddaddy of them all, it has served as a pilot program for similar schools at other institutions. It offers its members—about 650 retired professionals— more than 80 study groups in subjects ranging from Virginia Woolf to Highlights of Mathematics to Bridge for Beginners. Members may also enroll in one regular daytime New School course each semester.

For information: Institute for Retired Professionals, New School for Social Research, 66 W. 12th St., New York, NY 10011; 212-741-5682.

ACADEMY OF LIFELONG LEARNING

For information: University of Delaware, 2800 Pennsylvania Ave., CED, Wilmington, DE 19806; 302-573-4433.

CENTER FOR CREATIVE RETIREMENT

For information: Long Island University, Southampton, NY 11968-4198; 516-283-4000.

CENTER FOR LEARNING IN RETIREMENT

For information: University of California Extension Center, 55 Laguna St., San Francisco, CA 94102; 415-863-4518.

DUKE INSTITUTE FOR LEARNING IN RETIREMENT

Here some of the classes are led by peers, while others are taught by university faculty and local professionals.

For information: Duke University, Durham, NC 27708; 919-684-6259.

THE HARVARD INSTITUTE FOR LEARNING IN RETIREMENT

For information: Harvard Institute for Learning in Retirement, Lehman Hall B-3, Cambridge, MA 02138; 617-495-4973.

THE INSTITUTE FOR LEARNING IN RETIREMENT

For information: The American University, Nebraska Hall, 4400 Massachusetts Ave., NW, Washington, DC 20016; 202-885-3920.

A sampling of similar peer learning programs:

INSTITUTE OF NEW DIMENSIONS

Palm Beach Junior College's peer learning school is held at three locations in Florida: Palm Beach Junior College Central Campus in Lake Worth; North Campus in Palm Beach Gardens; and Florida Atlantic University Center in West Palm Beach. Here the yearly fee is very low (currently $25), and you may take an unlimited number of courses. Student body numbers at about 15,000!

For information: Institute of New Dimensions, Palm Beach Junior College, 3160 PGA Blvd., Palm Beach Gardens, FL 33410; 305-622-2440, ext 307.

NOVA COLLEGE INSTITUTE FOR RETIRED PROFESSIONALS

For information: Nova College Institute for Retired Professionals, 3301 College Ave.,Fort Lauderdale, FL 33314; 305-475-7036.

THE PLATO SOCIETY OF UCLA

For information: The Plato Society of UCLA, 10995 Le Conte Ave., Los Angeles, CA 90024; 213-825-7917.

PROFESSIONALS AND EXECUTIVES IN RETIREMENT

For information: Hofstra University, 1000 Hempstead Turnpike, Hempstead, NY 11550; 516-560-6919.

TEMPLE ASSOCIATION FOR RETIRED PROFESSIONALS

For information: Temple University, 1619 Walnut St., Philadelphia, PA 19103; 215-787-1505.

MORE GOOD WAYS TO GET SMARTER

CHAUTAUQUA INSTITUTION

The "55 PLUS" Weekends and the Residential Week for Older Adults are sponsored by Chautauqua Institution. For 115 years, people have been going to the shore of Lake Chautauqua, 75 miles south of Buffalo, New York, to a sort of cultural summer camp in a Victorian village. The 856-acre hilltop compound offers a wide variety of programs, including summer weeks and off-season weekends especially for the over-55 crowd. These programs get filled up far in advance, so if you're interested, don't waste a moment.

The weekends each have a specific focus; for example, the U.S. Constitution, natural history, world population, experiencing the arts, trade relations with Japan. They include discussions, workshops, lectures, films, recreational activities, and evening entertainment and are led by professionals. Housing and meals are provided in a residence hall.

The Residential Weeks for Older Adults are similar but longer and include lodging and meals as well as admittance to other goings-on at the center. It's all quite cheap: the current weekly cost of tuition, room, meals, and planned activities for a week amounts to about $225 and for a weekend about $75.

For information: Helen Overs, Program Center of Older Adults, Chautauqua, NY 14722; 716-357-6200.

CLOSE UP

An "educational vacation" in Washington, DC, Close Up is designed for people who are at least 50. The idea is to give you a whole week of firsthand access to "inside" Washington. Activities include two or three seminars a day with key Washington personalities (senators, White House officials, foreign ambassadors, reporters, and others) on topics of current concern; daily briefings for background information; motorcoach tours of the city; a day on Capitol Hill; all meals, many at interesting restaurants; an evening at the theater; daily workshops to discuss issues and events; a banquet; and scheduled free time. You'll lodge in a good hotel.

All this, available to both groups and individuals, is remarkably inexpensive. That's because the weeks are offered in the spring and fall by the Close Up Foundation, a nonprofit, nonpartisan organization that has brought more than 160,000 people of all ages to Washington to study government "on location," in cooperation with the American Association of Retired Persons (AARP).

For information: Close Up Foundation, Dept. POA, PO Box 100, Arlington, VA 22210; 1-800-232-2000 (in Alaska and Virginia, call collect at 703-892-5428).

THE COLLEGE AT 60

Part of Fordham University and located at the Lincoln Center campus in New York City, the College at 60 offers credit courses in liberal arts subjects such as history, psychology, philosophy, economics, literature, and computers, taught by Fordham faculty members. Included are a lecture series and the use of all college facilities. After taking four seminars, students receive a certificate and are encouraged to enter the regular Fordham University program.

Believe it or not, you are eligible for the College at 60 if you are over 50.

For information: The College at 60, Fordham University at Lincoln Center, 113 W. 60th St., New York, NY 10023; 212-841-5334.

THE EDUCATIONAL NETWORK FOR OLDER ADULTS

This not-for-profit organization in Chicago, which charges nothing for its services, is a network of 65 colleges and universities, adult organizations, community centers, and associations. Its purpose is to help older people in the greater Chicago area find the educational and training programs they need.

ENOA's Resource Center will answer questions on anything "from getting a GED, vocational training and further academic education to finding a bridge group, getting a manuscript published, finding volunteer work, starting a new business, or locating financial-retirement planning seminars." In other words, it's there to help.

For information: The Education Network for Older Adults, 36 S. Wabash, Suite 624, Chicago, IL 60603; 312-782-8967.

ELDER COLLEGE AT HOFSTRA

These are one-week programs offered throughout the year for people over 60 who live close enough to commute to the school. You'll spend five days attending classes (recent classes have included Richard Rodgers: A Life in the American Musical Theatre; The Literature of the Holocaust; Art and Archaeology of Golden

Greece) from 9:00 A.M. to 3:00 P.M. and socializing with fellow students.
For information: Elder College at Hofstra, UCCE, 232 Memorial Hall, Hempstead, NY 11550; 516-560-5016.

THE NORTH CAROLINA CENTER FOR CREATIVE RETIREMENT

Designed to help the graying set forth on a fulfilling life when they no longer have to spend all their energies on their jobs, this is an unusual setup. For those over 50, it features eight components: a Pre-Retirement Institute to help people make wise decisions about when, where, and how to spend their retirement; the College for Seniors, with a range of courses within the University of North Carolina, including travel-study courses in many parts of the world; an institute that holds workshops on vital issues such as housing options and finances; a leadership program of accomplished people who provide their expertise to the community and the university; an educational health program; a service league; a council that provides consulting for small businesses; and a research institute. That's a big handful of programs put together for the first time under one umbrella.
For information: The North Carolina Center for Creative Retirement, University of North Carolina at Asheville, Asheville, NC 28804-3299; 704-251-6512.

UNIVERSITY SENIORS

Membership in this New York University program for people over 65 gets you two free university courses per semester and biweekly luncheon discussion sessions on subjects of current interest. Recent topics have included archaeological finds, myths and the Bible, and criminal behavior in America.

For information: University Seniors, NYU School of Continuing Education, 11 W. 42nd St., New York, NY 10036; 212-998-7130.

GETTING AN EDUCATION IN CANADA

Virtually every college and university in Canada offers free tuition to students over the age of 60 or 65, whether they attend classes part-time or full-time. Colleges of applied arts and technology generally offer postsecondary credit courses through their Departments of Continuing Education or Extension to seniors and charge a mere $5 or $10 per course. Aside from the nonexistent or low cost, seniors are treated just like the other students, have the same privileges, and must abide by the same regulations.

For information: Write to the registrar of the college you've chosen for information about its program or, for general information, to the Ministry of Colleges and Universities in your province.

Chapter Seventeen

Shopping for Breaks

Clever marketing experts have recently realized that the over-50s, a segment now growing three times faster than the rest of the country's population, is the next target market. We not only have more money to spend but are more inclined to spend it than younger consumers. On the other hand, we're a bunch of cautious consumers who know the value of a dollar and are always on the lookout for a bargain.

SAVING IN YOUR NEIGHBORHOOD

THE SILVER PAGES

If you want to know which merchants and other businesses in your own neighborhood will give you a decent break, simply look in *The Silver Pages*. This is a discount directory for people 60 or better, published by Southwestern Bell Media in more than 100 cities or areas around the country—and soon to be available in many others.

This directory can save you plenty of money and time because it lists businesses—from pharmacies to plumbers, dentists, bakeries, motorcycle shops, hospitals, TV repair shops, dress shops, attorneys, and fish markets—that offer you discounts or special deals of some variety such as free consultations or examinations, delivery service, or gifts.

The directory costs you nothing because it makes its revenue from the listed businesses. Once you are on the mailing list, you will automatically receive a new edition every year. To take advantage of the discounts or other perks, you will need a Silver Savers' Passport, an identification card that is also free and will be sent to you with the directory. It's valid wherever an edition of

The Silver Pages is published, in your city and others.

In addition to the listings, each directory contains a community resources guide, produced in cooperation with local agencies and filled with useful information about all special services and programs available to you in your area, whether local, regional, or national. **For information:** Call 1-800-252-6060, 8:00 A.M. to 4:15 P.M. CST.

READING FOR LESS

Join Waldenbooks' 60+ Book Club, which costs absolutely nothing and gets you handy discounts on new books. You can sign up at any of the 1,070 Waldenbooks stores across the country. Membership entitles you to discounts of up to 10 percent on books that cost up to $14.99 and 15 percent on books that cost $15 or more. You will also be able to pick up the club's *60+ Newsletter* free in the stores. This is an eight-page bimonthly publication that contains general articles and features books that are likely to be of special interest to you.
For information: The Waldenbooks 60+ Newsletter, 201 High Ridge Rd., Stamford, CT 06904.

SAVING MONEY IN THE STORES

A couple of large national department store chains offer some special services and enticements to shoppers over 50.

SEARS ROEBUCK & CO.

Sears started Mature Outlook several years ago as an over-50 club. Along with the club's other benefits, it offers sizable retail price cuts at Sears stores, which members get by cashing in special discount coupons good for a variety of products and services. The coupons come your way regularly once you've joined the organization and may be used in Sears stores in the United States and Canada. See Chapter 20 for the details on signing up with Mature Outlook.

MONTGOMERY WARD

Not to be outdone, Montgomery Ward has started its Y.E.S. (Years of Extra Savings) Discount Club, which aims to save you money in many directions after you hit the magic age of 50. As a member (membership costs $34.80 a year for you and your spouse), you receive a membership card, a Y.E.S. Discount Pass, and a quarterly magazine called *Vantage*. With the membership card and the pass in hand, you will get 10 percent off any merchandise (sale or non-sale) in Montgomery Ward stores every Tuesday. And, on Tuesdays, Wednesdays, and Thursdays, you will be entitled to 10 percent off auto service (wheel alignment, computerized engine analysis, oil change, installation of shock absorbers or struts, brake service, or tuneup).

In addition, the club has just launched a really innovative service, the Y.E.S. Club Travel Service. You may make airline reservations via the travel service and, on your return from your trip, you send in a claim form for a 5 percent rebate on the cost of the tickets. The deal is even better on hotel/motel or car-rental reservations—on these, you get a 10 percent rebate.

For information: Montgomery Ward Y.E.S. Discount Club, 200 N. Martingale Rd., Schaumburg, IL 60194; 1-800-421-5396 (in Illinois, 1-800-621-4797).

A NEW LEASH ON LIFE

Through **Purina Pets for People**, an ingenious program funded by Ralston Purina, local humane organizations provide pets for people over 60 at no initial cost to the recipients. The program pays for adoption fees, initial veterinary visits, spaying or neutering, and a starter kit of pet supplies, and contributes a supply of Purina Dog Chow or Cat Chow pet food. The program is designed to rescue a passel of homeless pets, a lot of them grown and trained, and give them to people who'd like the company. Of course, prospective owners must pass their local shelter's screening procedure to be sure they can provide the proper care.

For information: Purina Pets for People, Checkerboard Sq., 6T, St. Louis, MO 63164.

Chapter Eighteen
Taxes, Insurance, and Other Practical Matters

This chapter is not filled with great suggestions for having fun, but the information here may tip you off to some facts and benefits that are coming your way if you want them.

FEDERAL INCOME TAX

The new tax law no longer provides an extra exemption for those over 65 years of age. Instead, it gives you a larger standard deduction than younger people are entitled to, according to Richard Feuerstein, New York accountant. The standard deductions on the short income-tax form for everyone *under* 65 are $5,000 for married couples filing jointly, $2,500 each for married people filing separately, $3,000 for single people, and $4,400 for single heads of households.

However, if one spouse of a couple filing jointly is over 65, the standard deduction has been increased (by $600) to $5,600; if both are over 65, it is increased (by $600 twice) to $6,200. For a married person filing separately, the deduction increases (by $600) to $3,100. A single person over 65 may now deduct $3,750 ($750 more than those who are younger); and a head of a household's deduction is increased (by $750) to $5,150. None of this applies, of course, if you itemize your deductions.

Beyond 1988, the standard deductions and the extra values for over-65s may be adjusted for inflation.

SALE OF PRINCIPAL RESIDENCE
You can save money on taxes if you are (or your spouse is) 55 when you sell the home you have owned and lived in as a principal residence for at least three years out of

the five-year period ending on the date of the sale. You may elect to exclude from your gross income for federal tax purposes up to $62,500 if you are married and filing separately or $125,000 if you are single or married and filing a joint return.

Before you decide to take advantage of this, however, be sure to discuss it with a tax consultant because this exclusion may be used only once in your lifetime and you may be better off saving the privilege for a later home sale.

GETTING HELP WITH YOUR TAX RETURN

Tax assistance is usually available to you free through the Internal Revenue Service or other private and public organizations. Check your area's *Silver Pages* for the appropriate addresses and telephone numbers. Or call your local tax department.

Better yet, contact the Tax-Aide service provided by American Association of Retired Persons (see Chapter 20) which now has more than 8,000 sites around the country where volunteer tax counselors assist low- and moderate-income taxpayers over 60 to complete their forms. Watch your local newspaper for the office nearest you or write to Tax-Aide Section, AARP, 1909 K St. NW, Washington, DC 20049.

AUTO AND HOMEOWNER'S INSURANCE

Mature people tend to be good drivers, becoming a much better risk class as a group than the younger crowd. You tend to be more careful drivers, having shed most of your hot-rod habits by now, and drive fewer miles. Therefore, statistically, you have about 10 percent fewer accidents per year than other risk categories do.

This is the reason many insurance companies offer discounts once you hit the magic number of 50 or 55 or thereabouts.

Some companies even offer reductions in premiums for homeowner's insurance as well, figuring you have become a more cautious and reliable sort who takes good care of your property.

Although discounts are wonderful and we all love to get them, they are not the whole picture, according to consumer advocate Robert Hunter of The National Insurance Consumers Organization: "You should shop the bottom line rather than discounts alone, always considering what you pay for the coverage you get. If a company charges higher premiums than other companies for comparable coverage and then gives you a discount, you haven't profited at all. Go for the bottom line with a reputable company."

Because insurance regulations differ from state to state, a complete list of companies giving discounts for age is impossible to assemble. It is best to go through an insurance agent or your state's Insurance Department. The following, however, are some of the special offerings of major firms in many states.

AETNA
In most states, Aetna gives a discount of about 10 percent off the premium on liability and collision coverage to good drivers 55 to 64 and about 20 percent to those over 65. And, over 55, you also get approximately 40 percent off on comprehensive auto coverage (fire and theft). Driving must be for pleasure use only.

HOW TO SAVE YOUR LIFE

If you happen to have the misfortune of falling ill or having an accident while you're away from home, **MedicAlert** may save your health—or even your life. When you join this nonprofit foundation (lifetime membership costs $20), you receive a metal bracelet or neck chain engraved with your personal identification number and a 24-hour-a-day call-collect telephone number tied into a data bank in California. When you or medical personnel call the data bank, all of your backup medical information is provided along with names and telephone numbers of your physician, next of kin, people to notify in an emergency, and other relevant information. As a backup, you get a wallet card containing the same material.

If you want your bracelet or neck chain in gold or silver, it will cost you more.

(By the way, Saga Holidays [see Chapter 7] offers a card to carry with you on your travels that contains emergency information such as medical history, blood type, insurance coverage, prescriptions, etc. Members receive theirs free; others may get one for $5.)

For information: To register by credit card, call 1-800-ID ALERT. Or write to MedicAlert Foundation, PO Box 1009, Turlock, CA 95381.

ALLSTATE

Allstate gives a 10 percent discount across the board—for all coverage—on both auto and homeowner's policies to people who are at least 55 and retired.

CHUBB

Chubb's offer is 10 percent off for drivers over 50 on liability and collision coverage and a 20 percent discount on comprehensive. Cars must be used for pleasure only, and there may be no youthful drivers (under 25) in the household.

GEICO

Good drivers from ages 50 to 65, using their cars for pleasure only, are given a Prime Time Rating and a discounted premium. Over 65, you're back where you started, however. Homeowners over 50 and retired get a 10 percent discount.

COLONIAL PENN

This company gives a retirement discount if you use your car only for pleasure.

HARTFORD

The company that services American Association of Retired Persons (see Chapter 20) offers members of this organization a discount of about 10 percent for completing an accredited defensive-driving course and up to 10 percent for maintaining a safe driving record. There are also lifetime renewal agreements, credits for low annual mileage, and full 12-month policies.

On homeowner's insurance, Hartford/AARP offers 5 percent credit on your total premium at any age in most states if you are retired.

LIBERTY MUTUAL

Special discounted rates are given by Liberty Mutual across the board on automobile insurance for those over 65.

NATIONWIDE
Nationwide gives a discount of 10 percent on all automobile coverage for people 55 and over.

US F & G
This company offers a discount of approximately 10 percent on auto coverage for people over 65.

BANKING

Many banks offer special incentives and services to people over 55 or 60, ranging from free checking to free NOW accounts, elimination of savings-account fees, gifts, or special rates. Every bank and every state is different, so you must check out the situation in your community. Again, *The Silver Pages* can be helpful. But best is some careful comparison shopping to make sure you are getting the best deal available.

LEGAL ASSISTANCE

Call upon your local area senior agency, which is required by law to provide some legal assistance to older citizens. Yours may help you untangle some puzzling legal problems or, at least, tell you what services are available to you. Or contact the local bar association for information. It is quite possible that it operates a referral or pro bono program. Or, suggests the American Bar Association, ask your local Legal Services Program for help or referrals.

Chapter Nineteen

Volunteer Options for Great Experiences

There's no need to hang around letting your talents and abilities go to waste once you've quit working for a living. If, perhaps for the first time in your life, you now have hours to spare, maybe you'd like to spend some of them volunteering your services to good causes. There is plenty of work waiting for you. You can find it on your own, of course, but it may be simpler to use the resources of the many programs that are designed specifically to take advantage of your wisdom and experience.

But, first, keep in mind:

Remember, when you file your federal income tax, you are allowed to deduct unreimbursed expenses incurred while volunteering your services. These include transportation, parking, tolls, meals and lodging (in some cases), and uniforms.

The following programs and organizations are actively looking for you and will make a match between you and those who need your help.

RETIRED SENIOR VOLUNTEER PROGRAM

Part of the government's national volunteer agency AC-TION, RSVP serves as a referral and placement service, matching people over 60 with appropriate volunteer work. Operating through local nonprofit private organizations or public agencies, RSVP is tailor-made for each community. In other words, whatever needs doing in your neighborhood is what you'll have a chance to do. You may choose hotlines; provide counseling on drug abuse, nutrition, finances, taxes, home repairs, or wills; or work in crime prevention, home care, or support groups.

For information: Contact your local or regional RSVP or ACTION office or ACTION, 806 Connecticut Ave. NW, Washington, DC 20525; 1-800-424-8867.

KNITTERS, STITCHERS, AND CARVERS, UNITE!

Elder Craftsmen encourages and advises people over 60 who want to make and sell their own handcrafts. A nonprofit organization operating for more than 30 years, it runs a retail shop in New York that sells most handwork on consignment, with 60 percent of the price going to the artist. Sometimes, however, it provides patterns and materials to skilled workers who work at home to produce specific items in quantity, in which case the craftspeople are paid by the piece. It also offers training courses for representatives of agencies and community groups and serves as an advisory group when needed.

For information: The Elder Craftsmen, Inc., 135 E. 65th St., New York, NY 10021; 212-861-5260.

THE SERVICE CORPS OF RETIRED EXECUTIVES

SCORE—which now includes ACE (Active Corps of Executives)—is a national organization of both active and retired professionals and business executives who offer their expertise free of charge to small businesses. SCORE counselors, who include lawyers, business executives, accountants, engineers, managers, journalists, and other specialists, provide management assistance and advice to small-business people who are going into business or who are already in business but need expert help.

With a current membership of more than 12,000 men and women, SCORE has about 400 chapters all over the mainland United States as well as Puerto Rico, Guam, and the Virgin Islands. Funded and coordinated by the government's Small Business Administration, it is operated and administered by its own elected officials.

For information: Contact your local U.S. Small Business Administration office or SCORE, 1129 20th St. NW, Suite 410, Washington, DC 20036; 1-800-368-5855.

AARP VOLUNTEER TALENT BANK

This public service was organized by AARP, the vast over-50 club (see Chapter 20), to help those who wish to serve others. Says a spokesperson, "People over 50 have a lifetime of experience and skills which can apply to a variety of volunteer interests," and the Talent Bank puts people and work together. After you complete a questionnaire about your personal background, interests, and skills, the information is matched by computer with opportunities for volunteer work within American Association of Retired Persons or by referral to other organizations in your own community.

For information: AARP Volunteer Talent Bank, 1909 K St. NW, Washington, DC 20049.

PEACE CORPS

No doubt you've always thought the Peace Corps was reserved for young idealists right out of college. The truth is that it's a viable choice for idealists of any age.

There is no upper age limit for acceptance into the Peace Corps, and since its beginning in 1961 thousands of Senior Volunteers have brought their talents and experience to developing countries in Latin America, the Caribbean, Africa, Asia, and the Pacific. To become a Senior Volunteer, you must be a U.S. citizen and meet basic legal and medical criteria. Some assignments require a college or technical-school degree or an experience equivalent. Married couples are eligible and will be assigned together.

What you get in return is the chance to travel, an unforgettable living experience in a foreign land, basic expenses, and housing, plus technical, language, and cultural training. And you will have a chance to use your expertise constructively in fields such as agriculture, engineering, math/science, home economics, education, skilled trades, forestry and fisheries, and community development.

For information: Peace Corps, Room P-301, Washington DC 20526; 1-800-424-8580, ext. 93.

VOLUNTEERS IN TECHNICAL ASSISTANCE

VITA provides another avenue for helping developing countries. A nonprofit international organization, VITA provides volunteer experts who respond—usually by direct correspondence—to technical inquiries from people in these nations who need assistance in such areas as small-business development, energy applications, agriculture, reforestation, water supply and sanitation, low-cost housing. Its volunteers also perform other services such as project planning, translations, publications, marketing strategies, evaluations, and technical reports and often become on-site consultants.

There is no minimum age, but you must be retired to serve. If you become a volunteer, you will not be paid, but will be reimbursed for your travel and living expenses.

For information: Volunteers in Technical Assistance, 1815 N. Lynn St., Suite 200, Arlington, VA 22209; 703-276-1800.

JOBS FOR EVERYBODY

If you're still in the market for a paying job, here are suggestions for your job search.

OPERATION ABLE

If you're over 45 and in the market for a job but don't know where to start looking for one, hook up with ABLE (Ability Based on Long Experience), a nonprofit umbrella organization affiliated with agencies that will match you with a likely employer—that is, if you happen to live in one of the communities where its network of independent agencies performs its magic: Chicago; Boston; Detroit; Los Angeles; New York; San Francisco; Little Rock, Arkansas; Brattleboro, Vermont; and, before long, Lincoln, Nebraska.

ABLE tries every which way to get you into the working world. It provides job counseling, on-the-job training, group training activities, and individual career assessment and guidance; teaches job-hunting skills; matches older workers with employers, operates a pool of temporaries; and offers myriad other services.

For information: Operation ABLE, 36 S. Wabash Ave., Chicago, IL 60603.

FOSTER GRANDPARENTS PROGRAM
This federal program sponsored by the government's national volunteer agency ACTION offers gratifying volunteer work to thousands of low-income men and women 60 and over, in communities all over the 50

FORTY PLUS CLUBS
Fifteen such clubs in the United States and one in Canada comprise this nonprofit cooperative of unemployed executives, managers, and professionals, men and women, 40 years of age or more. Their objective is to help members conduct effective job searches and find new jobs. There is no paid staff. The members do all the work and help pay expenses with their one-time charge of $800 (paid in installments). They must commit themselves to attend weekly meetings and spend at least two days a week working at the club and assisting others in their search for work.

In return, members are helped to examine their career skills and define their goals, counseled on résumé writing and interview skills, helped to plan marketing strategy, and given job leads. They may also use the club as a base of operations, with phone answering and mail service, computers, reference library.

Forty Plus Clubs exist at this writing in New York City and Buffalo, New York; Oakland and Los Angeles (with a branch in Laguna Hills), California; Denver (with subsidiaries in Fort Collins and Colorado Springs), Colorado; Chicago, Illinois; Columbus, Ohio; Dallas and Houston, Texas; Salt Lake City, Utah; Philadelphia, Pennsylvania; Washington, DC; Honolulu, Hawaii; and Toronto, Ontario.

For information: Addresses of the clubs and descriptive material are available from Forty Plus of New York, 15 Park Row, New York, NY 10038; 212-233-6086.

states, Puerto Rico, Virgin Islands, and the District of Columbia. The volunteers, who receive 40 hours of preservice orientation and training and four hours a month of in-service training, work with children who have special needs—boarder babies; troubled children; handicapped, severely retarded, abandoned, delinquent, abused, hospitalized, addicted, forlorn children who are desperate for love, care, and attention and do not get it from their families. They may work in hospitals, schools, homes, day-care programs, or residential centers.

Volunteers, who must be in good health although they may be handicapped, work 20 hours a week. For this, they receive, aside from the immense satisfaction, a tax-free annual stipend of $2,296, a transportation

McDONALD'S OVER-55 EMPLOYMENT PROGRAM

McDonald's, famous for its fast food, has started a program called McMasters designed to provide training and job placement for people 55 and older. When you sign on, you get four weeks of training, from 15 to 20 hours a week, under the supervision of a "job coach." The training consists of classroom instruction, floor demonstration, and supervised work on various job stations "including biscuits, salads, drive-thru, custodial maintenance, and hostess/host." At the end of the training period, graduates are mainstreamed into the work force at a McDonald's restaurant. So far, the McMasters program is operating in about 10 states with more in planning. Check with your local restaurant to see if the program is in the works in your vicinity.

allowance, hot meals while at work, accident and liability insurance, and annual physicals.

For information: Contact your local senior agency or Foster Grandparents Program, ACTION, 806 Connecticut Ave. NW, Washington, DC 20525; 1-800-424-8867.

INTERNATIONAL EXECUTIVE SERVICE CORPS

IESC, organized and directed by U.S. business executives, is a nonprofit organization that recruits retired highly skilled executives and technical advisors to assist businesses in the developing nations. It is funded by the U.S. Agency for International Development (AID), overseas clients and foreign governments, and many American corporations.

After being briefed on the country and the client, volunteer executives travel overseas—with their spouses, if they wish—for projects that generally last two to three months. IESC pays for the couple's travel expenses and provides a per diem allowance.

For information: International Executive Service Corps, 8 Stamford Pl., Stamford, CT 06904-2005; 203-967-6000.

NATIONAL EXECUTIVE SERVICE CORPS

This nonprofit organization performs a unique service: it helps other nonprofit organizations solve their problems by providing retired executives with extensive corporate and professional experience to serve as volunteer consultants. Its services are offered in five basic areas—education, health, the arts, social services, and religion—and the assistance covers everything from organizational structure and financial systems to marketing and funding strategy. Volunteers' expenses are covered.

For information: National Executive Service Corps, 622 Third Ave., New York, NY 10017-6753; 212-867-5010.

ZOA RETIREES PROGRAM

This is not a tour but a three-month working visit to Israel. You'll be working four hours a day; the rest of the time, you take Hebrew classes, attend a lecture series, tour, visit local homes. To be eligible you must be over 50, physically capable of working at least four hours a day, and in good health. You'll stay in a hotel, get three meals a day, and spend 13 days of your time on short trips around the country.

The voluntary work possibilities include tutoring English, providing assistance to aged or ill people, gardening in parks, working at an army base, doing forestry, renovating public buildings, and aiding in a hospital.

For information: ZOA Retirees in Israel Program, 4 E. 34th St., New York, NY 10016; 212-481-1500.

Chapter Twenty

The Over-50 Organizations and What They Can Do for You

When you consider that there are more people in this country over the age of 55 than there are children in elementary and high schools, you can see why we have powerful potential to influence what goes on around here. As the "demographic discovery of the decade," a group that controls most of the nation's disposable income, we've become an enormous marketing target. And, just like any other group of people, we've got plenty of needs.

A number of organizations in the United States and Canada have been formed in the last few years to act as advocates for the over-50 crowd and to offer us special deals and services. Here is a brief rundown on them and what they have to offer you. You may want to join more than one of them so you can reap the benefits of each.

THE AMERICAN ASSOCIATION OF RETIRED PERSONS

The biggest, oldest, and best known of all such organizations is AARP, a huge club with a vast array of services and programs. With more than 26 million members (6,000 join every day), AARP is open to anyone over 50, retired or not, and wields amazing power in the marketplace and among the nation's policy makers. Only two national magazines go to more people than its bimonthly *Modern Maturity*.

For a yearly membership fee of $5 (and that includes a spouse), AARP offers so many things that you are likely to stop reading before you get to the end of the list. But here they are:

▶ Supplemental health insurance at group rates provided by Prudential. All members are guaranteed eligibility.

▶ A nonprofit, mail-order pharmacy service, the largest in the world, that delivers by mail.

▶ Discounts at more than 15 major hotel and motel chains and resorts and on auto rentals from Avis, Hertz, and National rental agencies.

▶ A money fund in government-backed securities and six mutual funds.

▶ A travel service that offers preplanned tours, cruises, special-event programs "around the world or around the corner," and hosted living abroad, designed especially for mature voyagers (see Chapter 5).

▶ A specially priced motoring plan, provided by Amoco Motor Club, that gets you emergency road and towing service, trip planning, and other benefits.

▶ Auto and homeowner's insurance, via the Hartford Insurance Group, at a discount.

▶ *Modern Maturity* magazine, a bimonthly, full of general articles and useful information, plus a monthly news bulletin.

▶ A national advocacy and lobbying program to develop legislative objectives and priorities and represent the interests of older people at all levels of government, plus volunteer legislative committees that are active in every state.

▶ More than 3,500 chapters with a range of activities and volunteer projects, from teaching to helping out at the polls.

▶ Volunteer-staffed programs such as tax-preparation assistance, driver retraining, widowed-persons counseling, and Medicare assistance.

▶ Special service programs in such areas as consumer affairs, legal counseling, tax information, housing and health advocacy, women's activities, and crime reduction.

▶ The Institute of Lifetime Learning, a national clearinghouse for educational programs for mature people (see Chapter 16).

▶ Free publications on a vast number of subjects relevant to your life.

▶ And even more.

For information: AARP, 1909 K St. NW, Washington, DC 20049.

MATURE OUTLOOK

Only four years old, this membership organization has already attracted almost a million dues-paying members. You must have a U.S. address to be a member. Owned by Sears, the country's largest retailer, this club specializes in discounts, some of them hefty, on products and services in its stores, plus myriad other benefits for people over 50. The annual fee of $7.50, which includes your spouse, also gets you discounts on everything from travel to hotels and motels, used cars, prescriptions, eyeglasses, and lube jobs on your car.

Here's a quick look at this club's services and benefits:

▶ *Mature Outlook Magazine*, which you get every other month. This is a readable, colorful, artfully designed magazine with articles and columns full of information you can use.

▶ *Mature Outlook Newsletter*, which you receive in the alternating months, also a source of useful facts and tips.

▶ Discount coupons from Sears that give you savings on both regular and sale-priced items. The coupons are inside each issue of the newsletter.

▶ Automotive service: a coupon book redeemable at Sears Automotive Centers giving you discounts on various maintenance jobs for your vehicle.

▶ Travel service (see Chapter 5) for domestic and international travel packages and individual tours designed with over-50s in mind, provided by Trans National. Also special savings on last-minute space.

▶ Discounts of 10 to 25 percent on several major hotel and motel chains and on car rentals from Budget/Sears, Hertz, and National.

▶ Mail-order pharmacy discounts through Walgreen's, discounts on eyeglasses, and no-fee traveler's checks with home delivery.

▶ A 10 percent discount on any regularly priced menu item, from steak to coffee, at Ponderosa Restaurants, and at Holiday Inn restaurants.

▶ $300 off the regular retail price on used cars purchased from any corporate Hertz Used Car Sales.

▶ Ten percent off the membership charge for the Allstate Motor Club.

▶ And more.

For information: Mature Outlook, PO Box 1208, Glenview, IL 60025-9935; 1-800-366-6330.

CANADIAN ASSOCIATION OF RETIRED PERSONS

For $10 a year (including spouse), you can join CARP, a brand-new nonprofit association for Canadians over 50 (who make up almost a quarter of the country's population). Inspired by AARP, it provides you with discount rates on lots of good things, from health insurance to car rentals, hotels, theaters, and travel. It also sends you a quarterly newspaper called *CARP News*.

For information: CARP, 27 Queen St. E., Suite 304, Toronto, ON, Canada M5C 2M6; 416-363-8748.

NATIONAL COUNCIL OF SENIOR CITIZENS

An advocacy organization, NCSC lobbies on the local, state, and national level for legislation benefiting older Americans. With about 4.5 million members, it has carried on many successful campaigns in the areas of housing, health care, Social Security, and the like.

Although NCSC's major focus is its legislative program, it also has a local club network, social events, prescription discounts, group rates on supplemental health insurance, automobile insurance, and travel discounts, plus a newspaper that keeps you up to date on all of the above. Yearly dues are $8.

For information: National Council of Senior Citizens, 925 15th St. NW, Washington, DC 20005; 202-347-8800.

NATIONAL ASSOCIATION FOR RETIRED CREDIT UNION PEOPLE

Obviously, not everybody can join this club, but those who can get some good benefits. These include an attractive and useful magazine called *Prime Times* and

the *NARCUP Newsletter*; car-rental discounts; Medi-
care-supplement insurance; pharmacy discounts; lodging discounts at some Quality Inns, Ramada Inns, and
KOA campgrounds; and a motor club. Also, discounted
travel packages and tours.
For information: NARCUP, PO Box 391, Madison, WI
53701; 608-238-4286.

NATIONAL ASSOCIATION OF RETIRED FEDERAL EMPLOYEES

As you have probably gathered, this is an association of
federal retirees and families. Its primary mission is to
protect the earned benefits of retired federal employees
via its lobbying program in Washington. Membership
is $12 a year.
For information: NARFE, 1533 New Hampshire Ave.
NW, Washington, DC 20036; 202-234-0832.

OLDER WOMEN'S LEAGUE

The league is an advocacy group that works to improve
the lot of older women in this country—not an easy job.
Through a national organization and local chapters, it
provides educational materials, training for citizen advocates, informational publications and the like, deal-
ing with the important issues facing women as they
grow older. Membership fee is $10.
For information: Older Women's League, 730 11th St.
NW, Suite 300, Washington, DC 20001; 202-783-6686.

NATIONAL ALLIANCE OF SENIOR CITIZENS

This national lobbying organization with more than
two million members has a decidedly conservative tilt-

to-the-right bias, so people with middle-of-the-road or liberal views would not feel too much at home here. It works to influence national policy "on key issues of great importance to America and her future." For its dues of $10 a year ($15 for a couple), you receive newsletters and some benefits that include group insurance, prescription discounts, discounts on car rentals, lodgings, moving expenses, and an automobile club.

For information: National Alliance of Senior Citizens, 2525 Wilson Blvd., Arlington, VA 22201; 703-528-4380.

GRAY PANTHERS

With about 40,000 members of all ages, the Gray Panthers fight ageism and speak up for older Americans, reminding people "that people over 65 will not be pushed around by the Administration, not by callous landlords, not by nursing home profiteers, and not by an indifferent health care system. . . . Yet citizens past 65 are consistently the largest and most active voting block in the United States." Major areas of concern include Social Security, housing, nursing homes, Medicare, attitudes.

For information: Gray Panthers, 311 S. Juniper St., Philadelphia, PA 19107; 215-545-6555.

THE RETIRED OFFICERS ASSOCIATION

This group is open to anyone who has been a commissioned or warrant officer in the seven U.S. uniformed services. These folks receive a magazine whose articles are devoted to matters of special interest to them, and lobbying representation on Capitol Hill. They may also take advantage of several benefits, including discounts on car rentals and motel lodgings, a travel program with "military fares" to many overseas destinations, sports tournaments, a mail-order prescription program, group health and life insurance plans, and a car lease-purchase plan. Yearly membership fee is $16. TROA also has 375 autonomous local chapters that have their own activities and membership fees.

For information: The Retired Officers Association, 201 N. Washington St., Alexandria, VA 22314-2529; 703-549-2311.

Chapter Twenty-One

Practical Reading for People in Their Prime

To keep current on the latest opportunities for good deals and great adventures designed specifically for the mature set, you should do some reading. The following are some publications that consider you their audience. In them, you will certainly find news you can use and information that will be helpful in many areas of your life.

NEWSLETTERS

AARP News Bulletin is part of the AARP package, and you will get it regularly once you become a member. It alerts you to political issues affecting older Americans and the organization's current benefits and offers, gives handy tips and pertinent news. Contact AARP, 1909 K St. NW, Washington, DC 20049.

Mature Outlook Newsletter is a lively 16-page publication issued six times a year and sent to you when you join Mature Outlook. It is full of news, helpful advice, recommendations, and just plain interesting information about all manner of things. Contact Mature Outlook, PO Box 1205, Glenview, IL 60025; 1-800-336-6330.

The Mature Traveler, a monthly newsletter, aims at providing expert advice on saving money and avoiding trouble when you travel. It will keep you *au courant* on the latest travel offerings and current bargains for "older Americans." Cost is $21.97 a year. Order from GEM Publishing Group, PO Box 50820, Reno, NV 89513; 702-786-7419.

The Retirement Letter (Phillips Publishing Co.) is a monthly publication on making and saving money after you have retired. At $57 per year, it is full of useful tips and suggestions. Order from Peter A. Dickinson, Editor, 47 Chestnut St., Larchmont, NY 10538.

Travel Smart is not for mature travelers alone, but its purpose is to help its readers save money when they travel. In it, you will find many ways to do so, and always included are the latest special offers for people over 50. This newsletter makes a point of tipping you off to discounts, unusual travel ideas, and "deals of the month," sometimes special for its readers. For information about subscribing ($39 per year), contact Travel Smart, 40 Beechdale Rd., Dobbs Ferry, NY 10522.

Vital Connections, a quarterly newsletter put out by the Foundation for Grandparenting, works to "encourage understanding between the generations and enrich family connections." Membership in the organization (for a minimum $20 tax-deductible contribution) entitles you to an annual subscription to the newsletter. For details, contact Foundation for Grandparenting, PO Box 97, Jay, NY 12941; 518-946-2177.

MAGAZINES

Fifty Plus, published by Whitney Communications, is a general monthly magazine for an older audience, filled with articles of special interest to seniors. A well-edited publication, it is the only one that is not affiliated with a sponsoring organization. Available on the newsstands and by subscription, *Fifty Plus* will not only entertain you but also provides you with much useful information. Contact Fifty Plus, 850 Third Ave., New York, NY 10022; 212-593-2100.

Golden Years Magazine is a Florida publication distributed free in supermarkets, drugstores, and banks in that state. Or you may subscribe for $14.95 for 13 issues a year. Aimed at "Fantastic Floridians over 50," it tells you what's doing down there and how to take advantage of it. It also features general-interest articles on such subjects as travel, health, and real estate. Contact *Golden Years Magazine*, PO Box 537, Melbourne, FL 32902-0537.

Grandparents, a new quarterly magazine, addresses subjects of special interest to grandparents who want to develop a great relationship with their grandchildren near and far. Published by *Better Homes and Gardens*, it covers every possible aspect of grandparenting from knitting or cooking for your youngster to solving problems, sharing adventures, traveling together, playing together. It keeps you up to date on the best toys, games, books for young readers. Available on the newsstands and by subscription as well. Contact Grandparents, Meredith Corporation, 1716 Locust St., Des Moines, IA 50336; 515-284-3000.

Mature Outlook, too, is a genuine consumer magazine that is good reading. Part and parcel of your membership in the Sears organization for over-50s and paid for by your $7.50 yearly dues, its columns on money, health, gardening, and its articles on everything you might want to know about make it a valuable monthly arrival. See Chapter 20 for information about joining the organization and thereby getting the magazine.

Meridian, a magazine for Canadians who are 55 plus, is sent free to any Canadian who requests it (although there may soon be a subscription charge) and costs $10 a year for Americans. Its articles and editorial content are aimed at your age group. Contact *Meridian*, Troika Publishing Inc., Box 13337, Kanata, ON, Canada K2K 1X5.

Modern Maturity is the official AARP magazine, again part of your membership, paid for by your $5-a-year dues and sent to you regularly. This is a real magazine, with general articles, advertising, and columns, as well as information about AARP's many benefits and services. You will find lots to interest you here. See Chapter 20 for information about joining AARP.

Prime Times is a real magazine, a good one, although it is published for the members of the National Association of Retired Credit Union People which means most people haven't heard of it. It is a topical magazine with broad general appeal and includes well-written articles and special features that you will enjoy. It is also a superior magazine visually. As a nonmember of the sponsoring organization, you may subscribe anyway. Contact *Prime Times*, Box 391, 5910 Mineral Point Rd., Madison, WI 53701.

BOOKS

Access to the World: A Travel Guide for the Handicapped, by Louise Weiss (Henry Holt, $12.95), is an extremely useful book for physically handicapped travelers and their families, helping them to travel in comfort. Available in bookstores or ask the store to order from the publisher.

Bonnie Prudden's After-Fifty Fitness Guide, by Bonnie Prudden (Ballantine Books, $10.95), is written by the well-known fitness expert who states that being in good shape and pain free is half the battle in achieving a happy life after the midpoint. This book includes exercises, myotherapy (pain erasure) massage, and answers to many health problems, as well as the author's own down-to-earth philosophy. Available at bookstores or by special order.

The Complete Retirement Planning Book, by Peter A. Dickinson, discusses the five major areas of concern to potential retirees: health, finance, housing, legal matters, and leisure, and tells how to begin making plans early. $11.95 postpaid. Order from Peter Dickinson, 47 Chestnut Street, Larchmont, New York 10538.

Computers for Kids Over 60, by Greg Kearsley and Mary Furlong, research director of SeniorNet (see Chapter 16), this book helps you become computer literate, explaining what computers are and showing you how to use them to enhance your life. This book (Addison-Wesley, $9.95) and others in this field may be purchased at discounted prices from SeniorNet, Lone Mountain Campus, Rossi Wing, University of San Francisco, San Francisco, CA 94117-1080; 415-666-6505.

The Discount Guide for Travelers Over 55, by Caroline and Walter Weintz (E. P. Dutton, $7.95), is a state-by-state guide to senior discounts on hotels/motels, transportation, entertainment, museums, sights, and the like. Also has a section on foreign countries. Available from bookstores or ask the store to order from the publisher.

Fitness for Life: Exercises for People Over 50, by Theodore Berland (AARP Books), is just what it sounds like and will be a big help to people who want to remain in good condition. Order from AARP (see Chapter 20), or purchase from your bookstore.

Medical and Health Guide for People Over Fifty, by Eugene Nelson et al (AARP Books), helps you keep healthy, deal with medical problems, evaluate your health, change your habits. Order from AARP (see Chapter 20), or purchase at your bookstore.

Retirement Edens Outside the Sunbelt, by Peter A. Dickinson (AARP Books), tells the best places to retire in the states that don't fall into the Sunbelt. Order from AARP (see Chapter 20), or purchase at your bookstore.

Retirement Places Rated, by Richard Boyer and David Savageau (Rand McNally, $12.95), gives ratings to about 130 areas in the United States as retirement spots. It takes into account money, climate, personal safety, housing, leisure living. Available in bookstores, or ask the store to order it.

The Senior Citizen's Guide to Budget Travel in the United States and Canada, by Paige Palmer, shows you how to unearth low-cost transportation, accommodations, restaurants, etc. This and *The Senior Citizen's Guide to Budget Travel in Europe*, also by Paige Palmer, are inexpensive paperbacks that may be ordered from Pilot Books, 103 Cooper St., Babylon, NY 11702. Send for an order form.

BOOKLETS

Fifty-Plus Guidebooks are a series of booklets on subjects that may be dear to your heart now that you have reached the half-century mark. Titles include *Working in Retirement, Living Alone, Leisure and Your Successful Retirement, Housing.* Each costs $3.00 or $3.50, with special prices for multiple orders. For more information, see the magazine *Fifty Plus*, or write to 50-Plus Guidebooks, 850 Third Ave., New York, NY 10022.

Sunbelt Retirement, by Peter A. Dickinson (AARP Books), covers 500 communities in the 13 Sunbelt states from North Carolina to southern California to Hawaii in a state-by-state guide to retirement there. Order from AARP (see Chapter 20), or purchase at your bookstore.

Travel and Retirement Edens Abroad, by Peter A. Dickinson (AARP Books), lists the best places to retire throughout the world and a guide to getting there. Order from AARP (see Chapter 20), or purchase at your bookstore.

Travel Easy: The Practical Guide for People Over 50, by Rosalind Massow (an AARP Book, published by Scott, Foresman and Company, $8.95), gives you thoughtful, practical information about planning trips, preparing for them, and enjoying them, all the way from choosing a destination to packing to passports to touring safely. Order from AARP (see Chapter 20), or purchase from your local bookstore.

Index